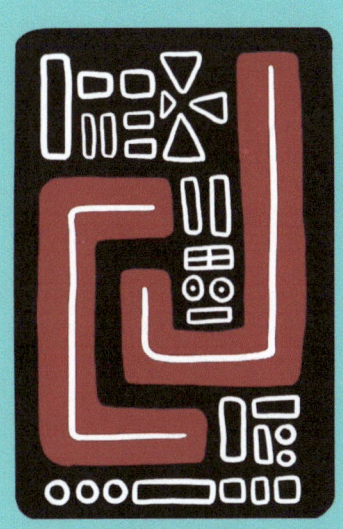

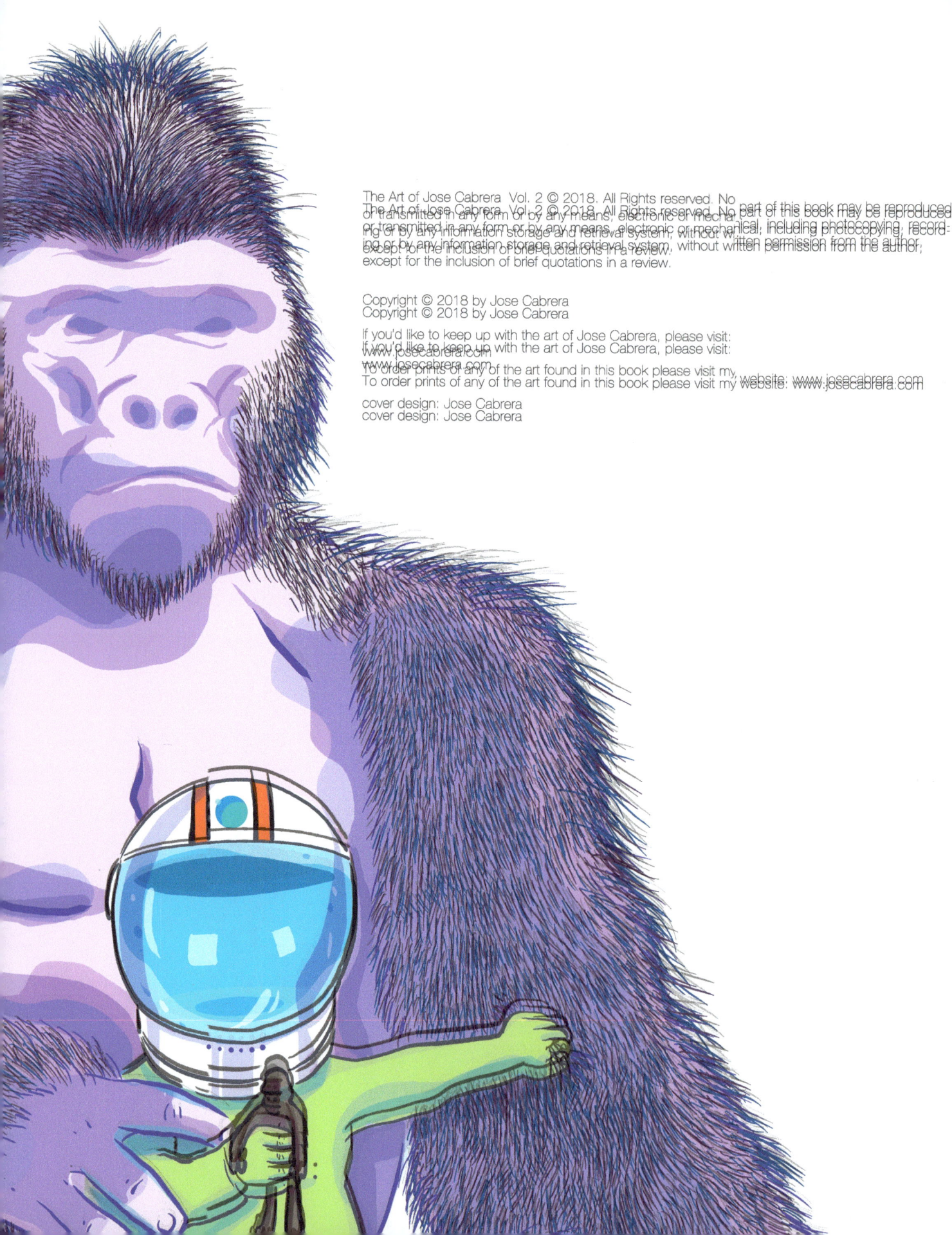

The Art of Jose Cabrera Vol. 2 © 2018. All Rights reserved. No part of this book may be reproduced or transmitted in any form or by any means, electronic or mechanical, including photocopying, recording or by any information storage and retrieval system, without written permission from the author; except for the inclusion of brief quotations in a review.

Copyright © 2018 by Jose Cabrera

If you'd like to keep up with the art of Jose Cabrera, please visit:
www.josecabrera.com
To order prints of any of the art found in this book please visit my website: www.josecabrera.com

cover design: Jose Cabrera

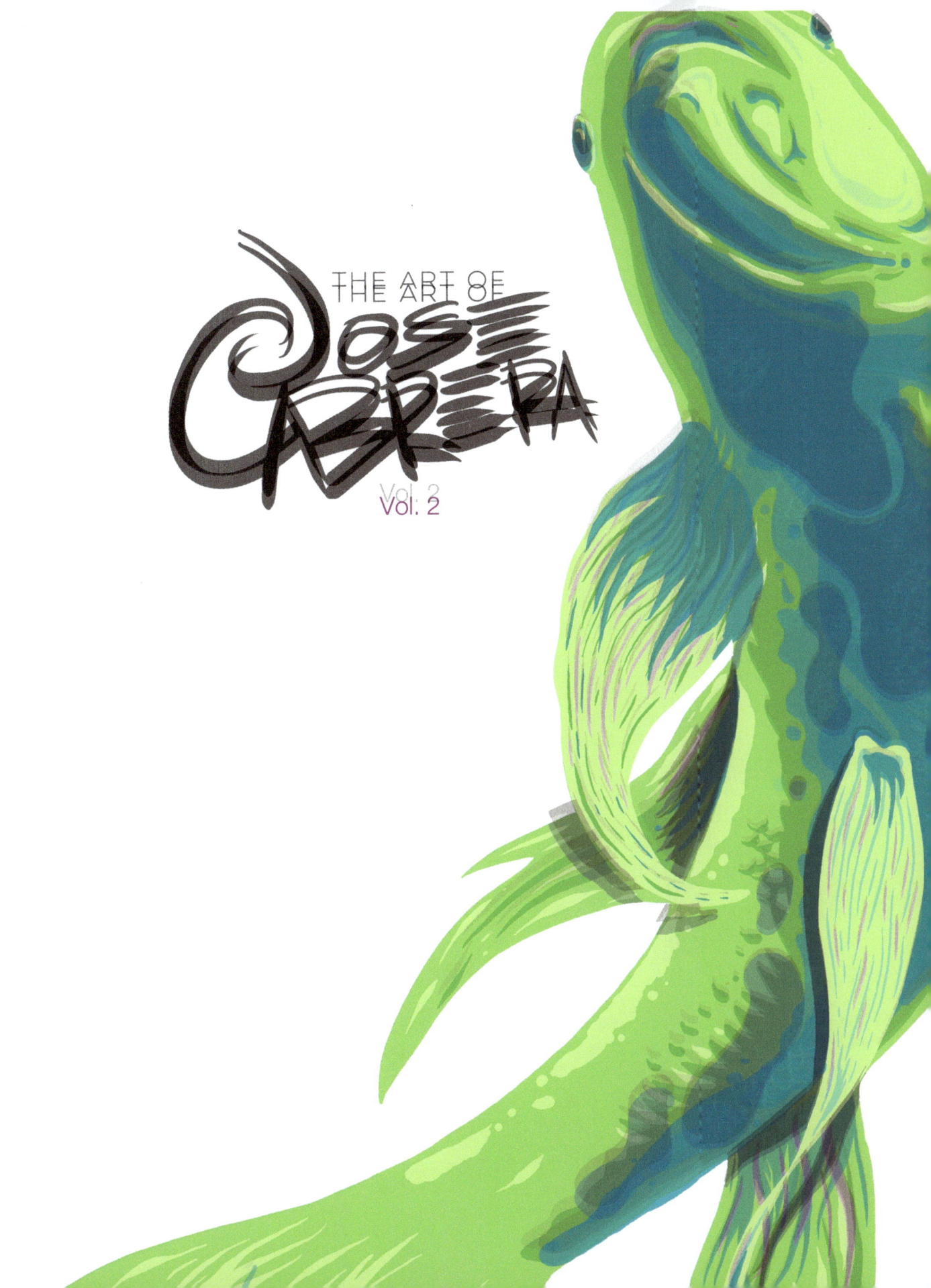

THE ART OF Jose Cabrera
Vol. 2

Cabrera's Speculative Sublimity

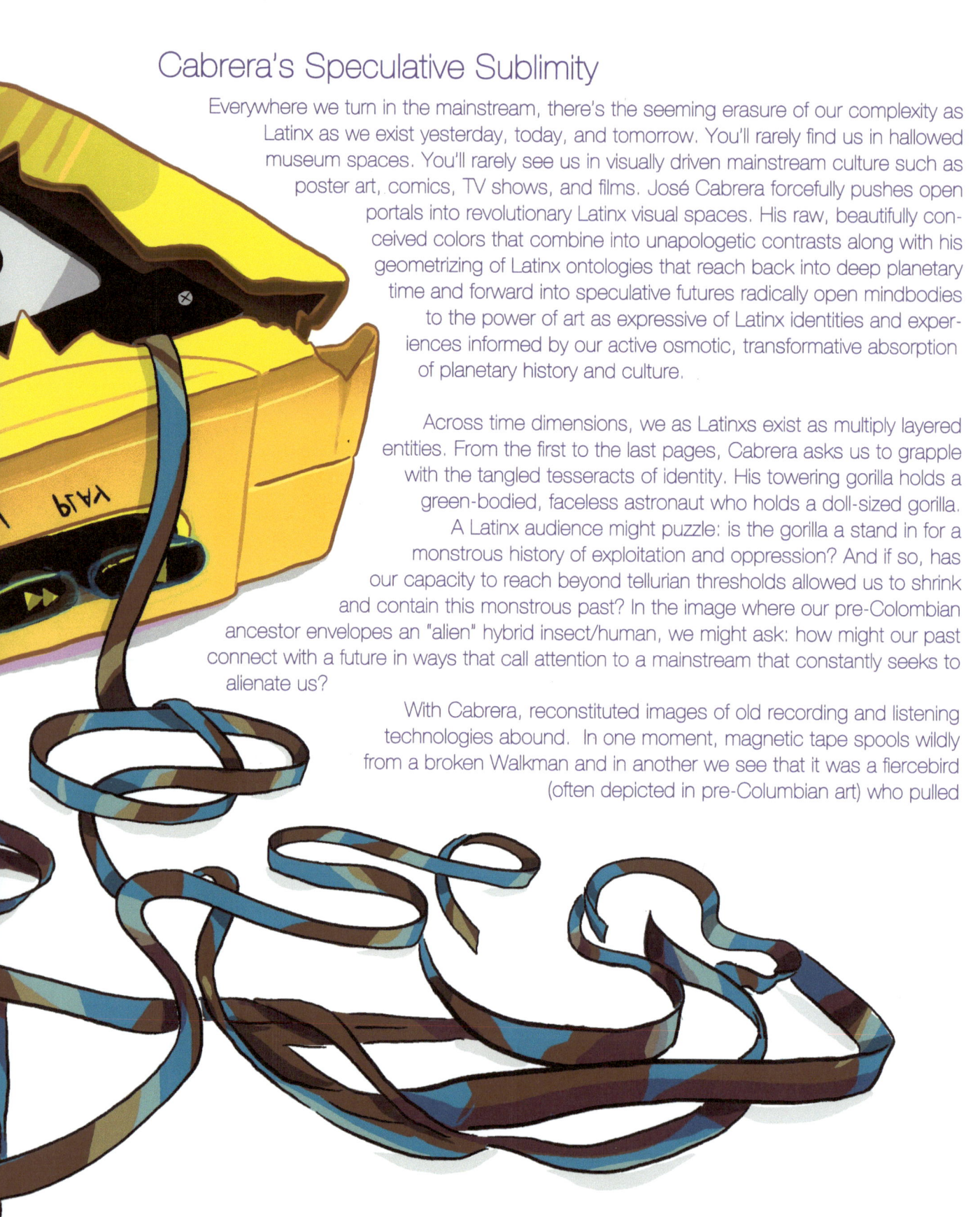

Everywhere we turn in the mainstream, there's the seeming erasure of our complexity as Latinx as we exist yesterday, today, and tomorrow. You'll rarely find us in hallowed museum spaces. You'll rarely see us in visually driven mainstream culture such as poster art, comics, TV shows, and films. José Cabrera forcefully pushes open portals into revolutionary Latinx visual spaces. His raw, beautifully conceived colors that combine into unapologetic contrasts along with his geometrizing of Latinx ontologies that reach back into deep planetary time and forward into speculative futures radically open mindbodies to the power of art as expressive of Latinx identities and experiences informed by our active osmotic, transformative absorption of planetary history and culture.

Across time dimensions, we as Latinxs exist as multiply layered entities. From the first to the last pages, Cabrera asks us to grapple with the tangled tesseracts of identity. His towering gorilla holds a green-bodied, faceless astronaut who holds a doll-sized gorilla. A Latinx audience might puzzle: is the gorilla a stand in for a monstrous history of exploitation and oppression? And if so, has our capacity to reach beyond tellurian thresholds allowed us to shrink and contain this monstrous past? In the image where our pre-Colombian ancestor envelopes an "alien" hybrid insect/human, we might ask: how might our past connect with a future in ways that call attention to a mainstream that constantly seeks to alienate us?

With Cabrera, reconstituted images of old recording and listening technologies abound. In one moment, magnetic tape spools wildly from a broken Walkman and in another we see that it was a fiercebird (often depicted in pre-Columbian art) who pulled apart this symbol of the West's straight-jacketing technologies used to contain Latinx voices, histories, and identities. Cabrera's reframing of containers of consumerism—from soup cans to Top Ramen® —demand an attentive refocus on histories of cultural containment. Cabrera's visuals, like the pre-Colombian codex, present a powerful counterpoint that emancipates our stories and persons. Pulling from Japanese (Tokugawa, shogun) and African (tribal carved masks) visual styles along with art traditions of the Americas (from tattoos to luchadores), Cabrera's willful geometrizing of elemental shapes such as water, fire, air, earth spin us into ever evolving vortices of time, place, and self. His hyperreal admixture of gasmasks, skeletal remains, chopped limbs reaching from mushrooms and worms with cherry blossoms and meditative mindful levitational states powerfully blur lines between life and death.

Cabrera's sharp eye, transmogrified figures and landscapes create visceral visualscapes that transform the 2D into multiplane, sublime Latinx edifices. Cabrera's paradoxes, antipathies along with harmonies and understandings thrust into the world the complex, affirmative ways that Latinx ontologies exist simultaneously as constructed in and through painful pasts as well as mindful, pleasurable presents and futures.

—**Frederick Luis Aldama,** *Latinx Superheroes in Mainstream Comics*

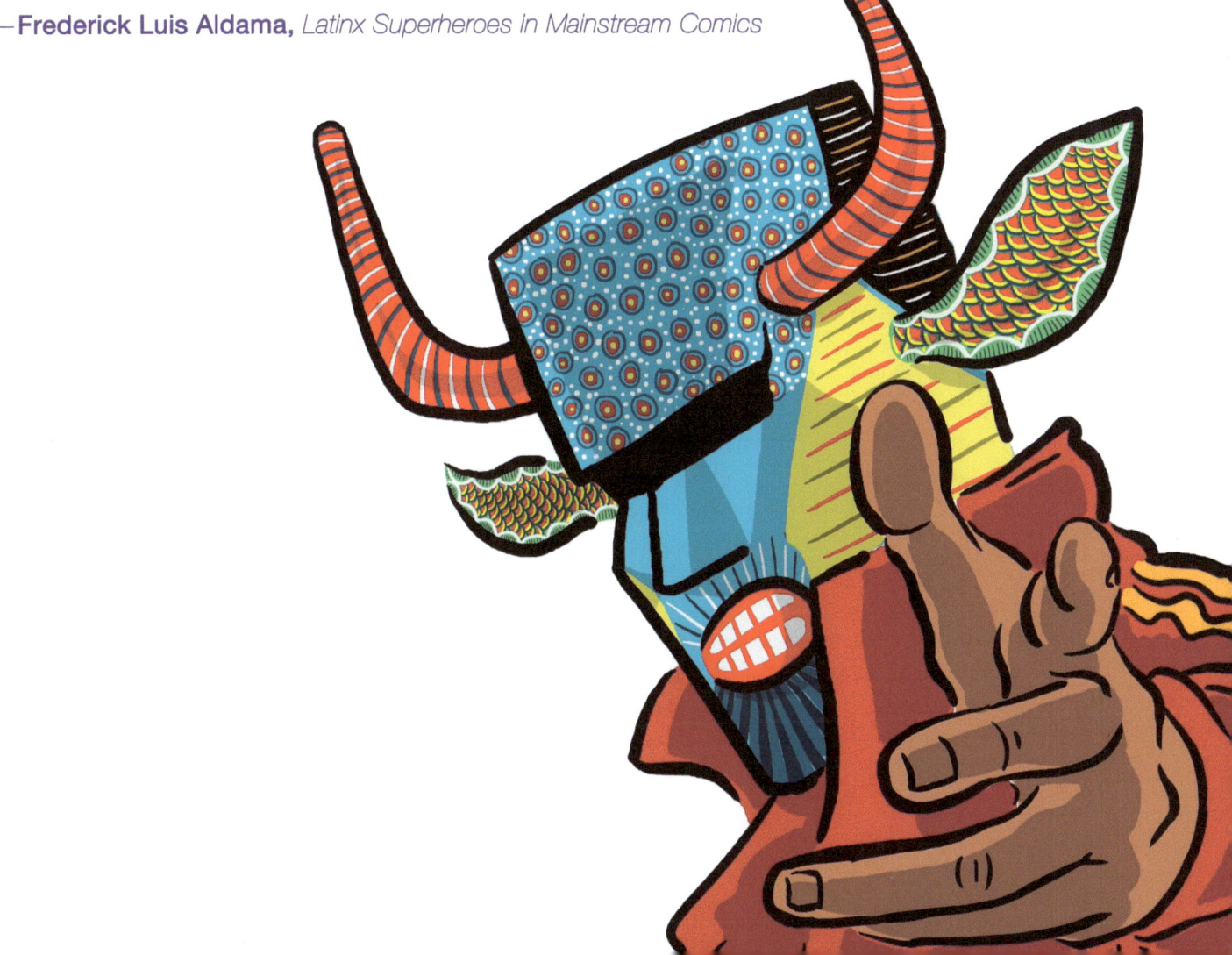

My Creative Flow

It's 5 in the morning and I am trying to decide whether to get up, put a cup of coffee on and do art. My body is screaming for more sleep, to dream a little more. But my drive to create wins out and I drag my feet like a sleepwalker over to the stove and boil some water. My wife and daughter are still sleeping so I tiptoe around like a thief. The coffee is strong and I pull out my iPad Pro. I use ProCreate to sketch out my ideas. Sometimes I get right to work, meticulously drawing the scales on Tyrannosaurus Rex for a children's book or doing the inks for an illustration. When I'm ready to color, I transfer the inks to my iMac in the living room, making sure to take my coffee. ProCreate can't handle the number of layers I use to color (about 50 on average). But my trusty desktop has the horse power (12 gigs of ram and 1 terabyte of hard drive space) for me to lay down the dozens of colors and transparencies. I have a very good relationship with photoshop and have been using it since the 90's. Coloring my work is a long process. On average it takes me about 30 to 40 hours for one art piece. The feathers on the crow show the level of detail I focus on. When I worked on "Los Elementos," specifically Fire, it was well over 45 hours. Some people say that digital art is cheating, but I say it's even more challenging because of the limitless options you have. I've embraced digital as my main medium for art making. I keep my skills honed by going to a live model class from time to time.

People ask me where I come up with my ideas and I'd like to say that it comes easy but it doesn't. Recently, I've looked through Pinterest to see what other artists are doing. There is some amazing art out there that is mind blowing and I get inspiration and even lift a composition or two that I like. I find that it isn't just about how well you draw but how you can mesh different ideas. Some illustrators can have strong design backgrounds and get an idea across so elegantly. I like the illustrations of Christoph Niemann who is well known for his New Yorker covers. He has an ability to play with abstraction and yet gets to put a smile across your face. And then there is the work of Ken Taylor who reimagines movie posters with bare monochromatic colors and slays me with his ornamental details and amazing compositions. Mouth watering. I'm also a big fan of local LA artist Tanner Goldbeck (we went to college together) and following his work over the decades. I remember handing in illustration assignments we stayed up all night doing. They weren't very good. And now he's opening up at Art galleries all over LA with these incredible ginormous pieces that take your breath away.

I truly believe that being an artist depends on putting yourself out there. There is this philosophical idea that artists and creatives alike ponder; *is it art if it stays in your closet?*
GO MAKE ART AND SHOW US!

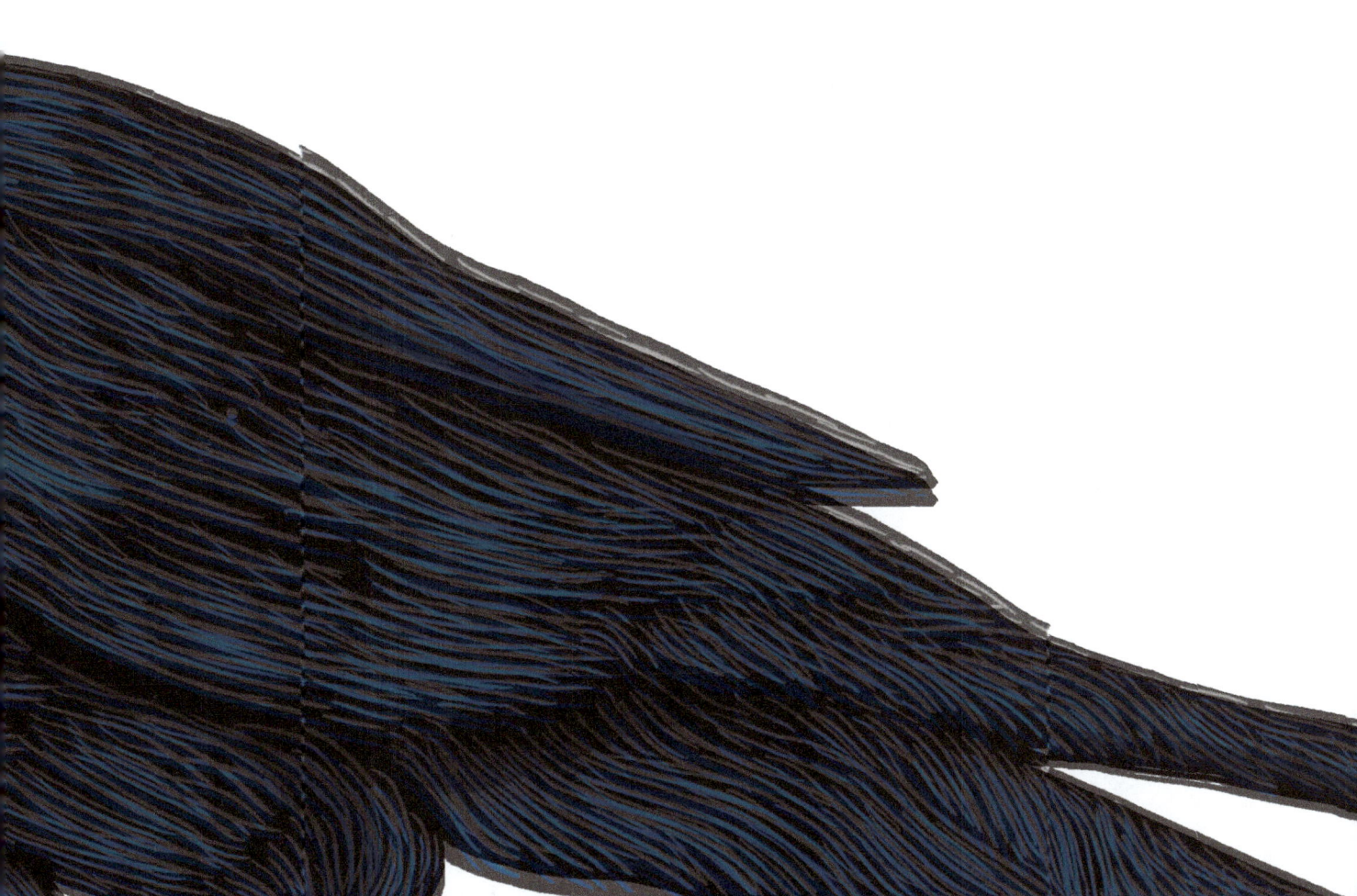

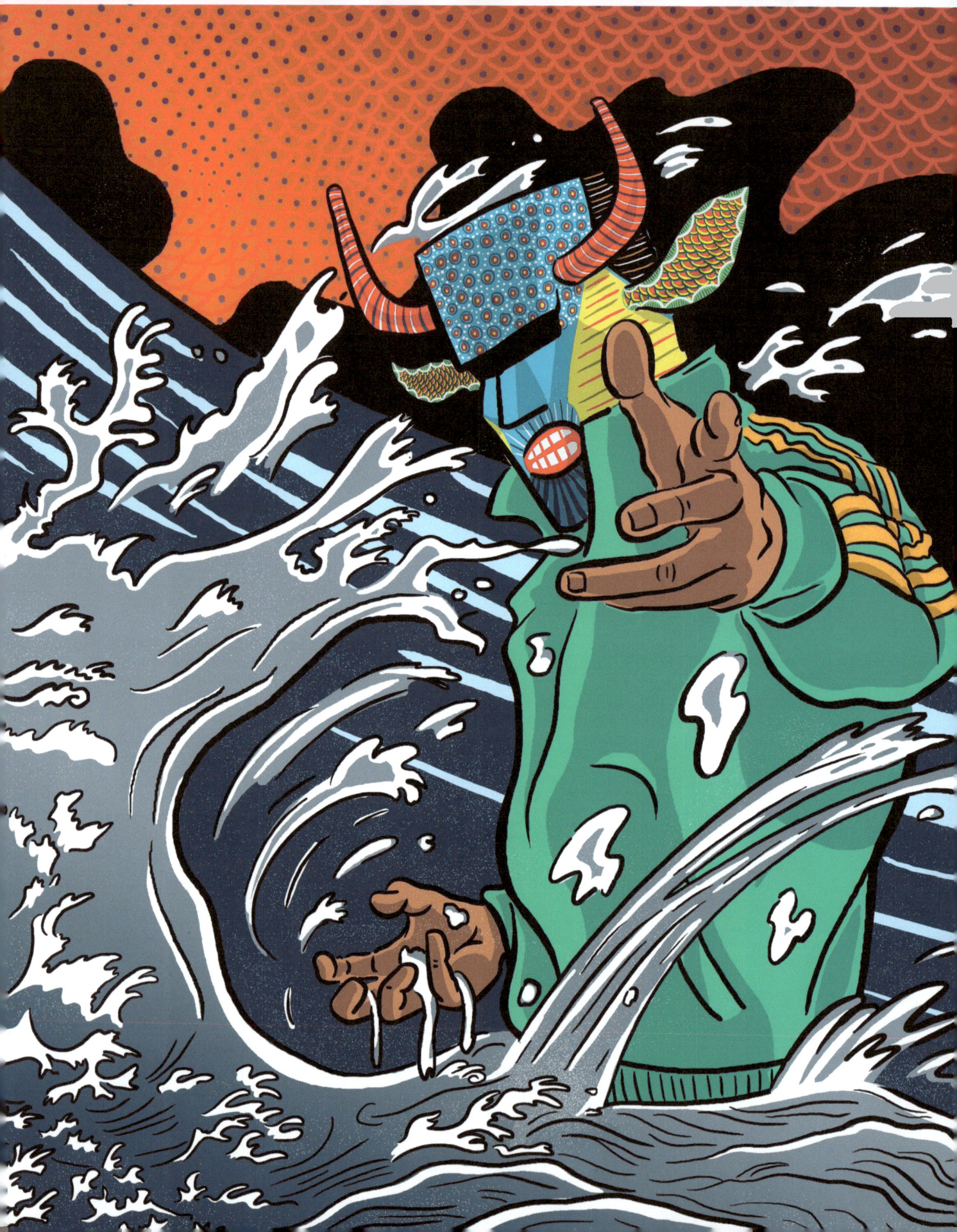

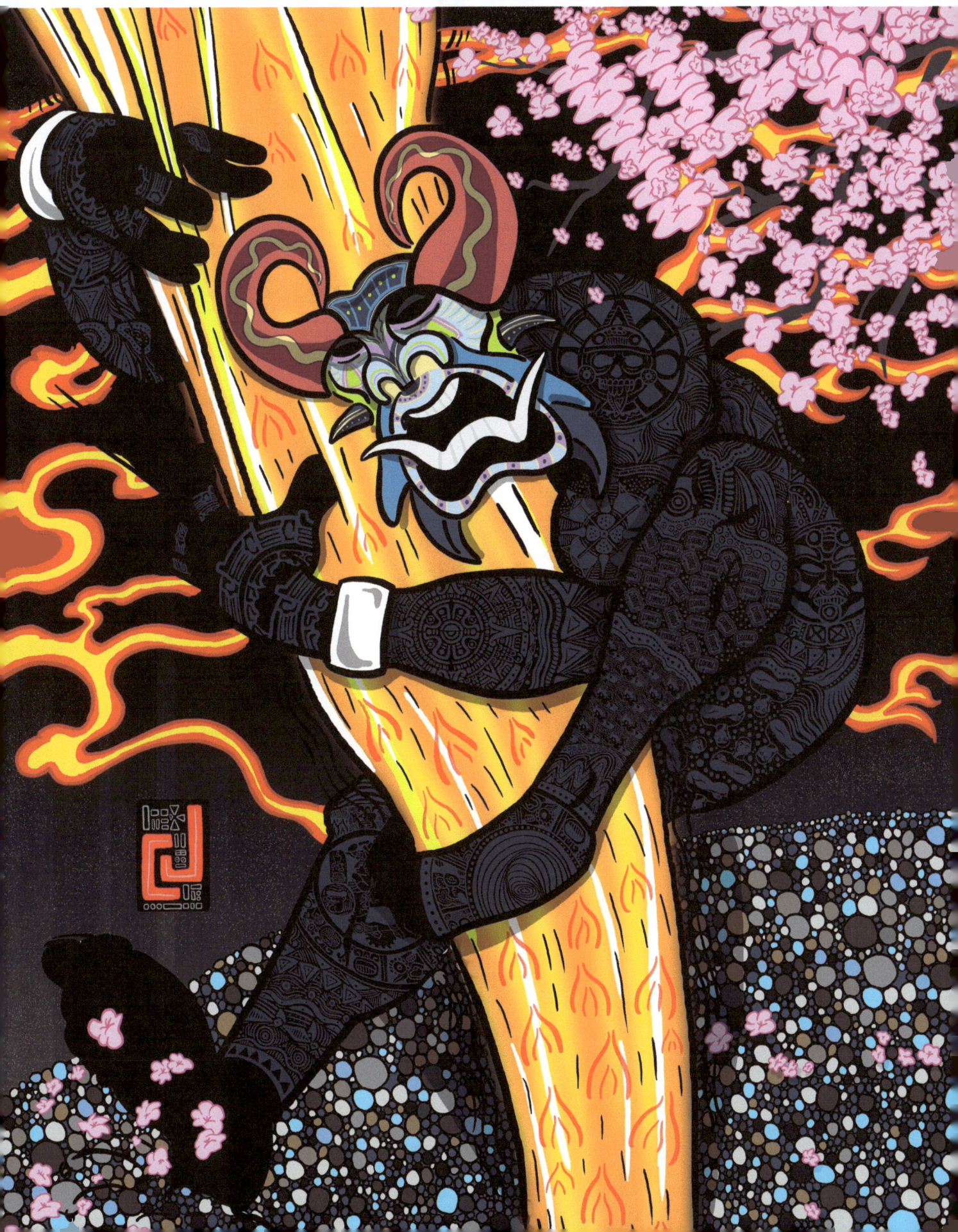

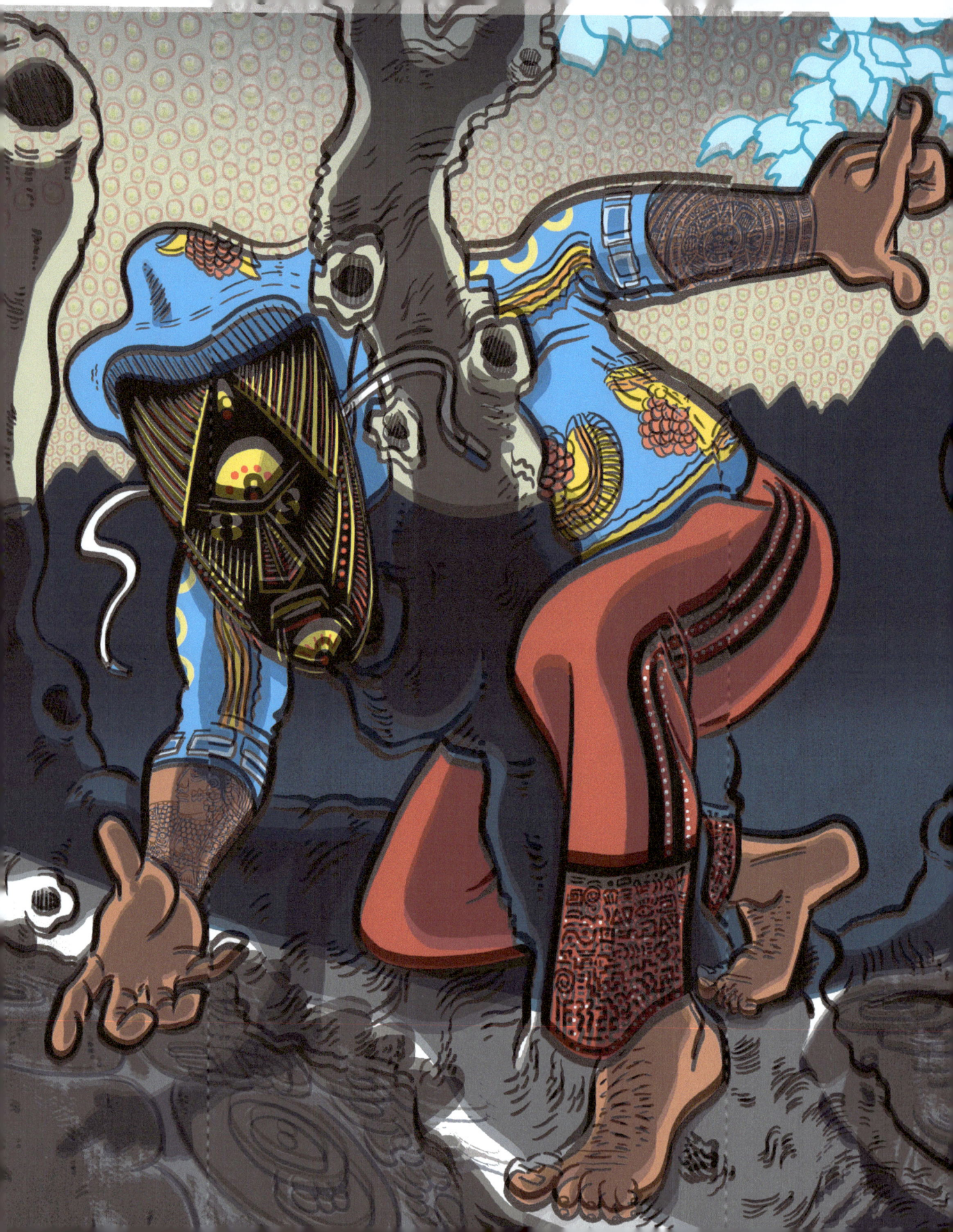

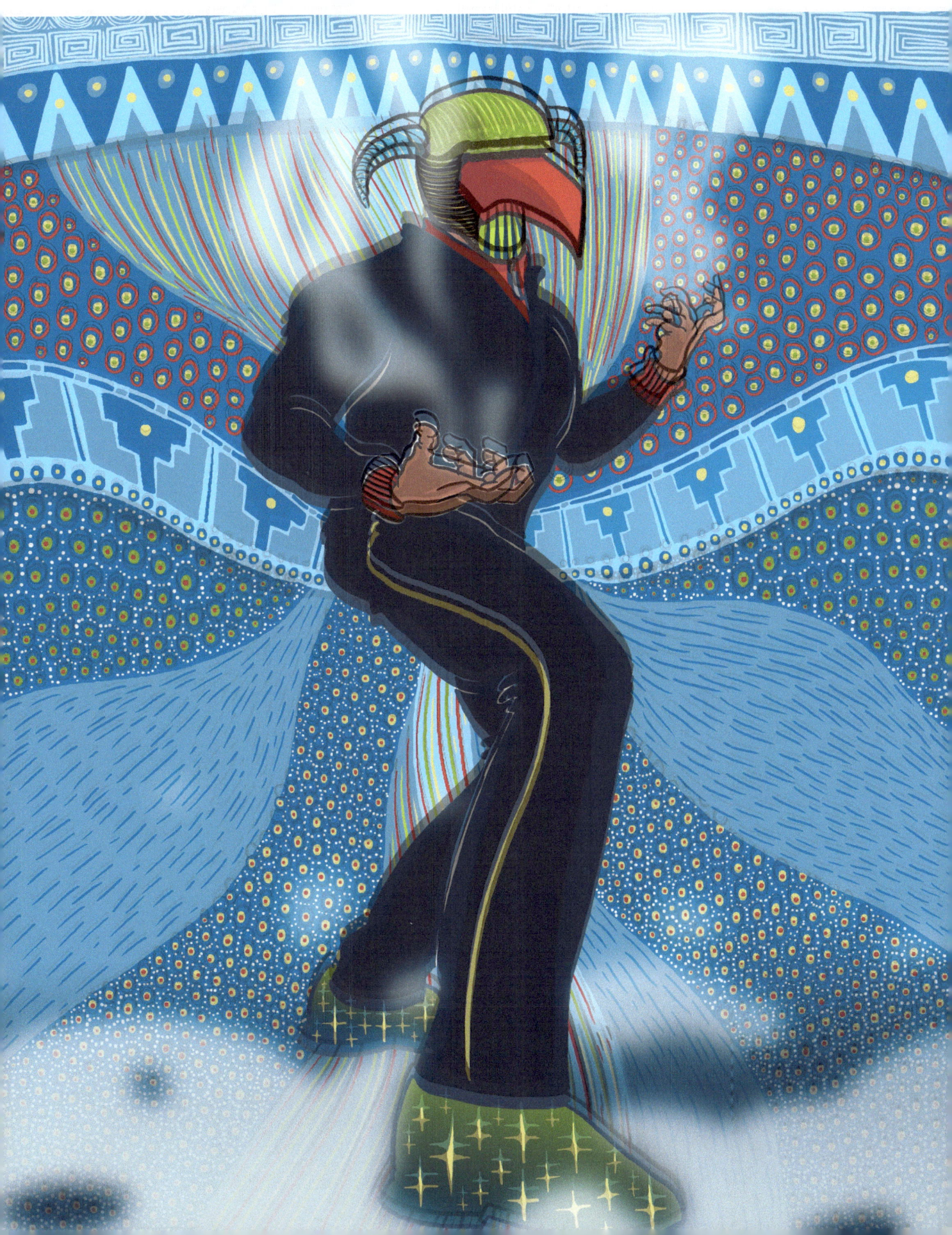

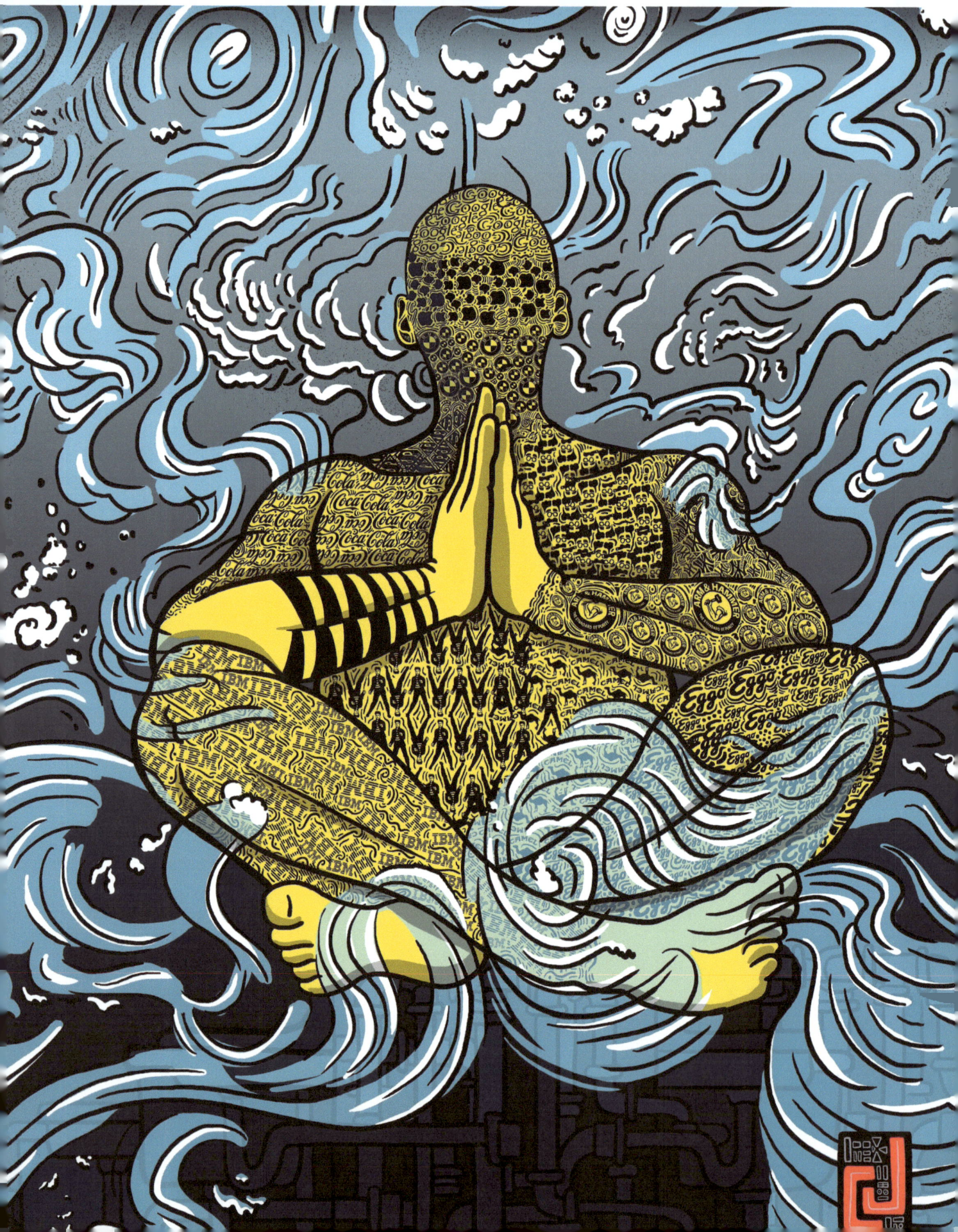

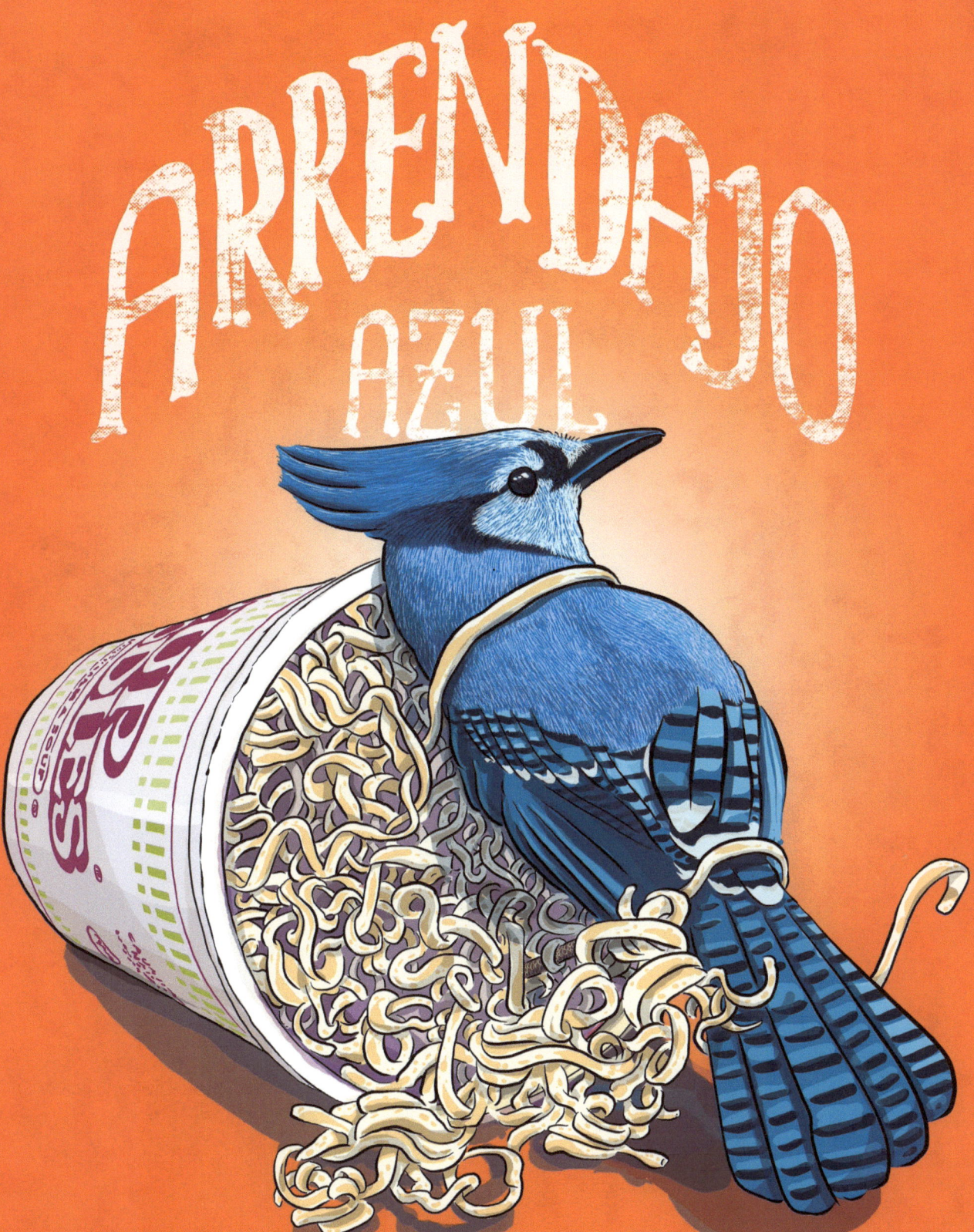

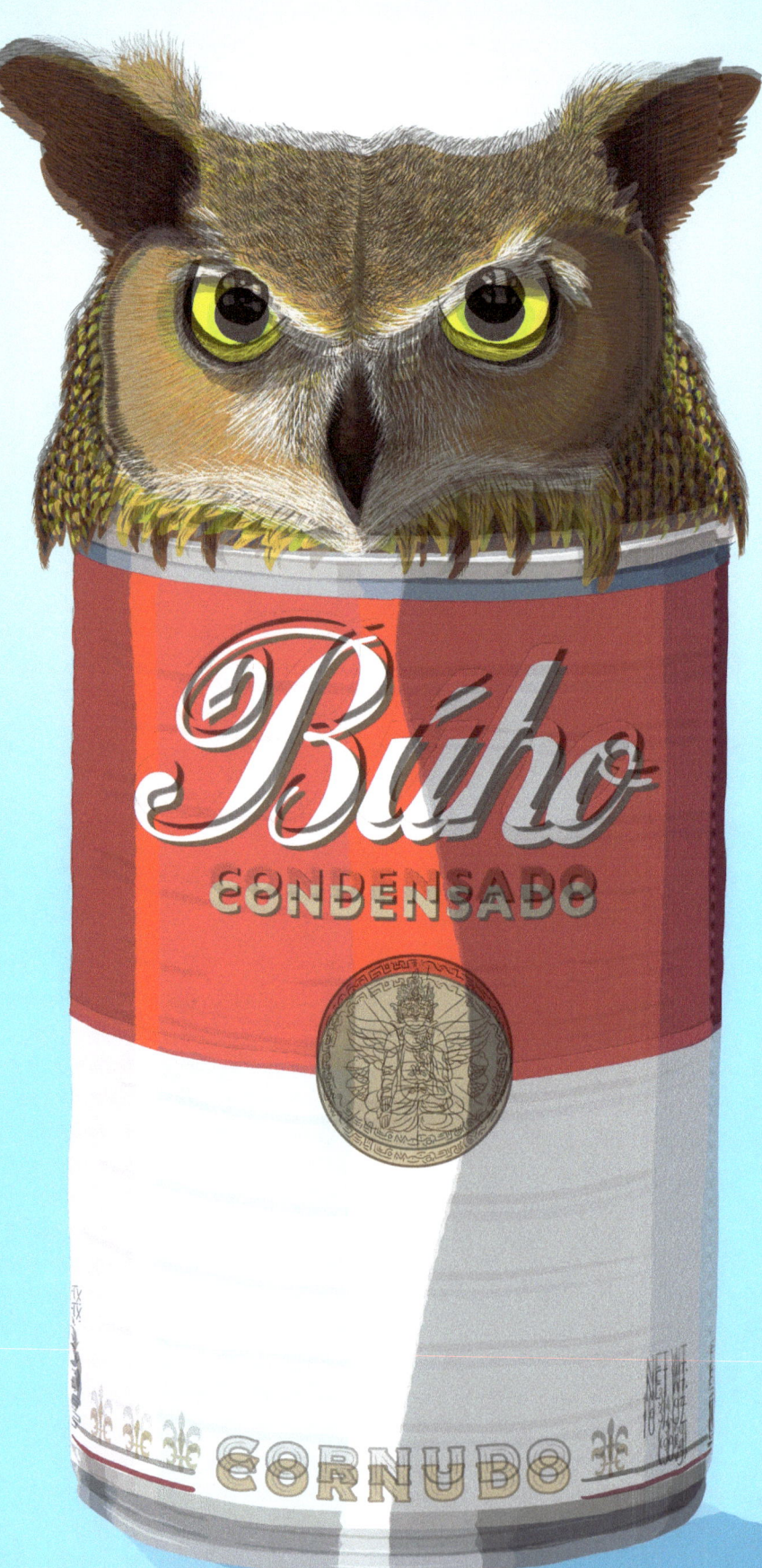

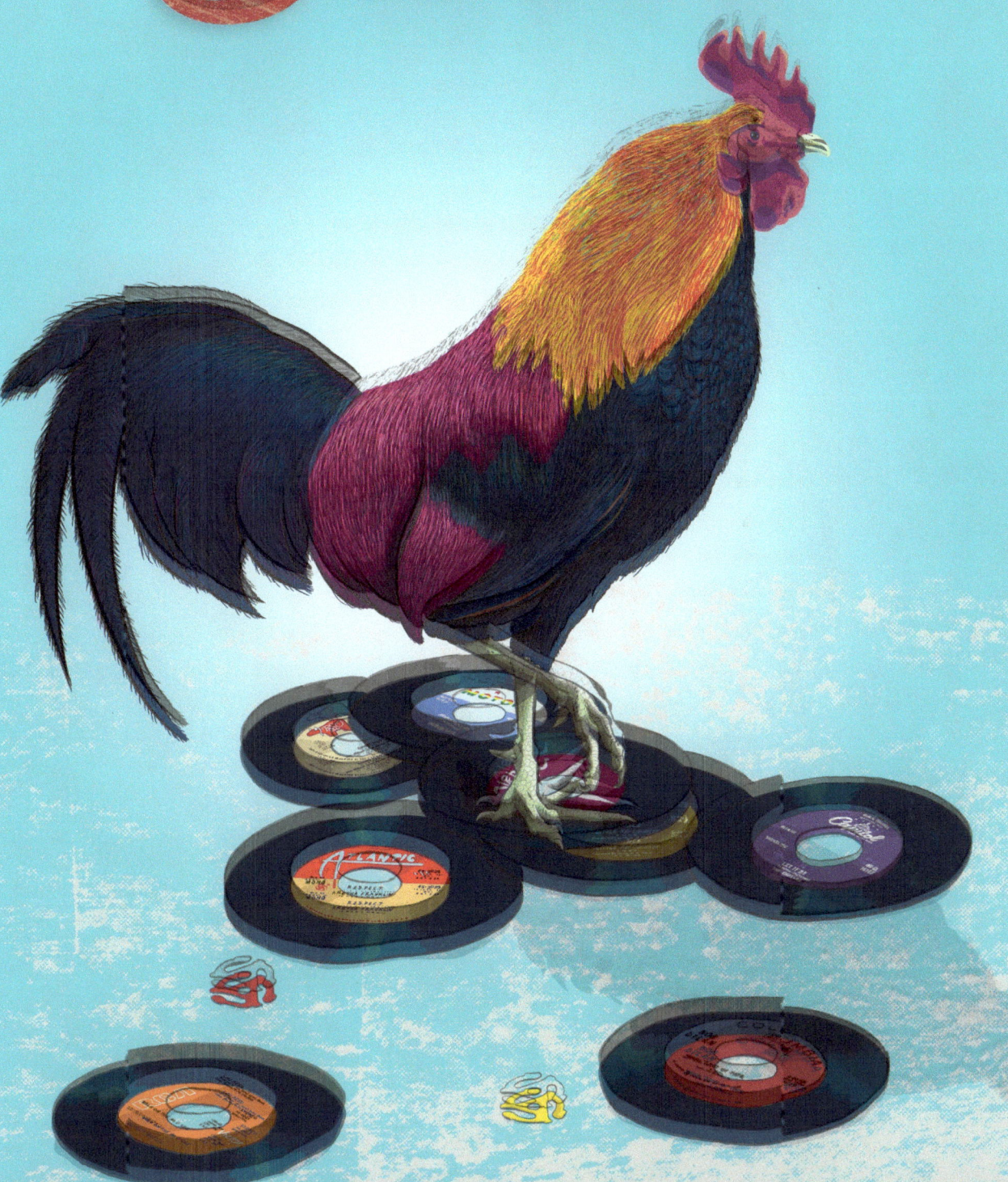

el Cuervo

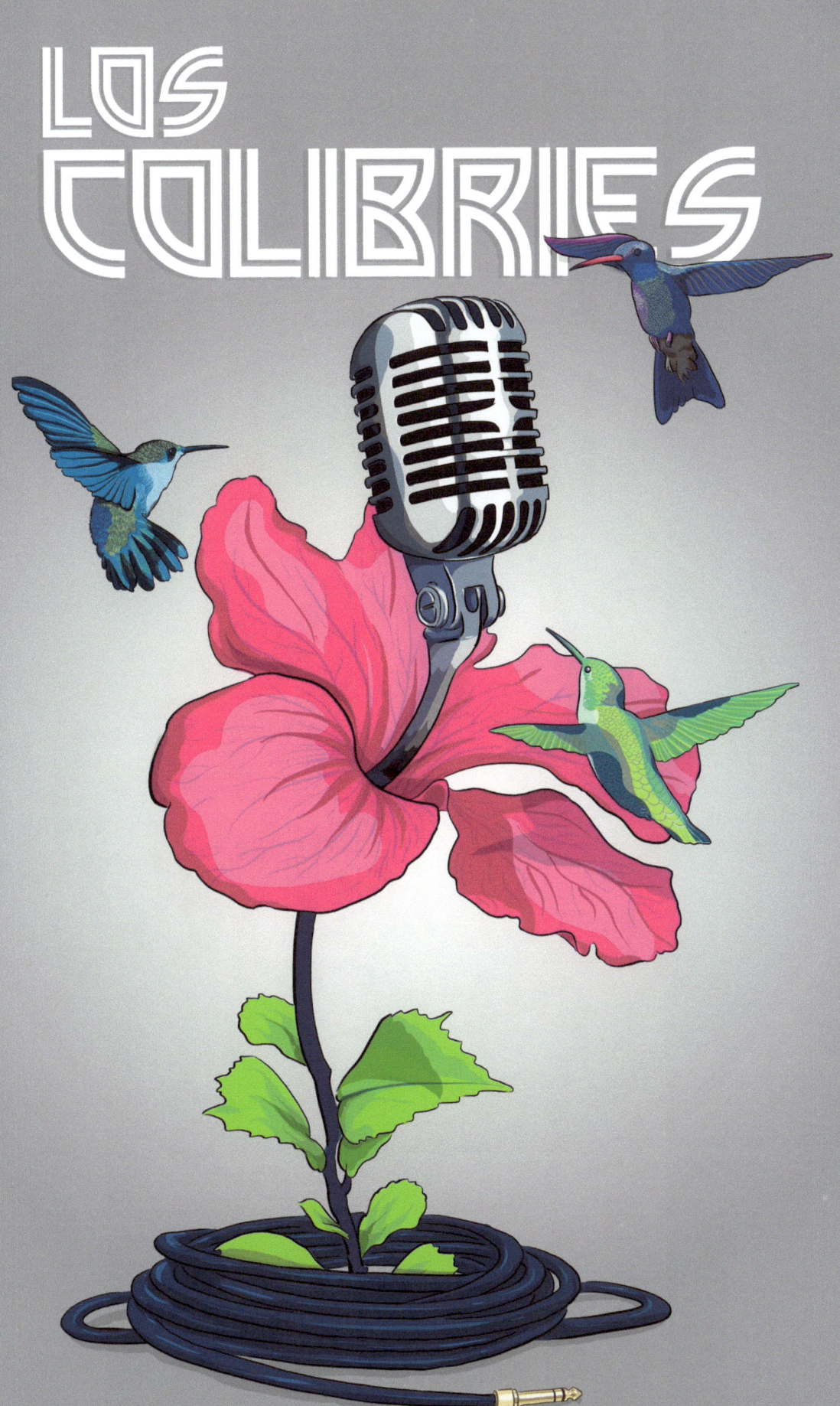

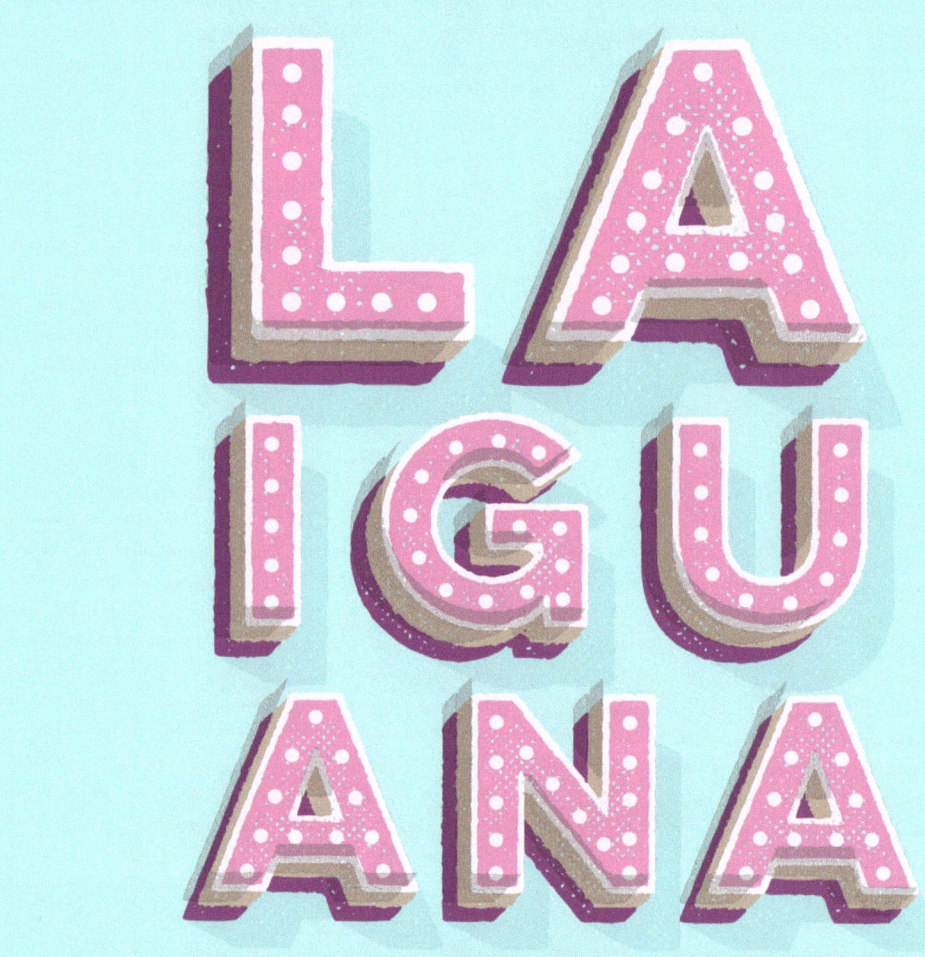
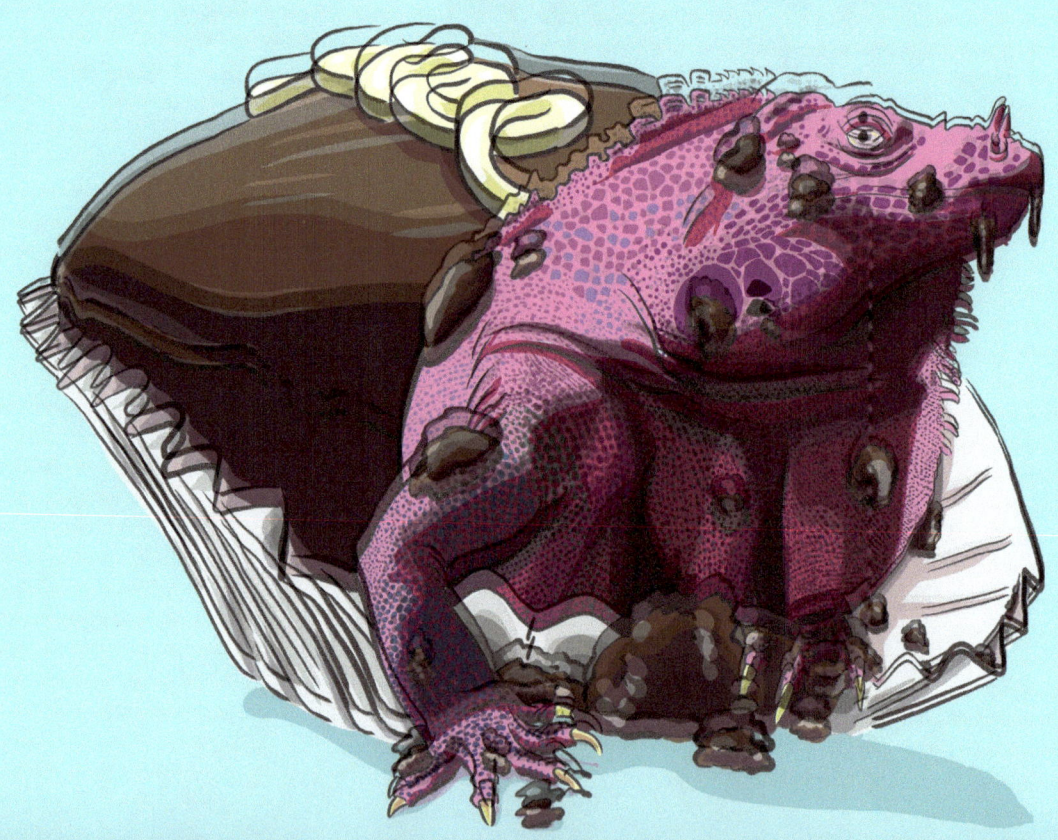

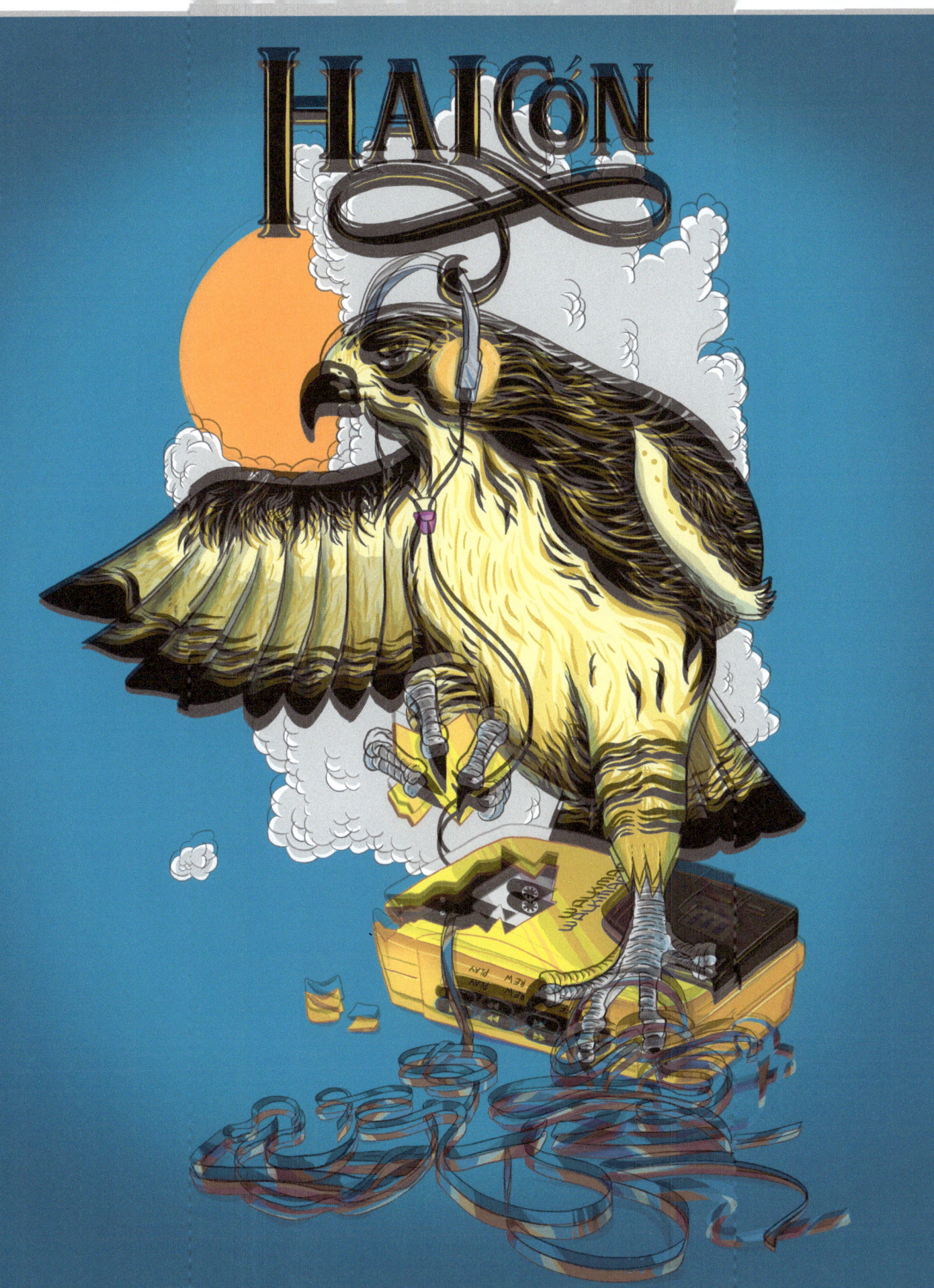

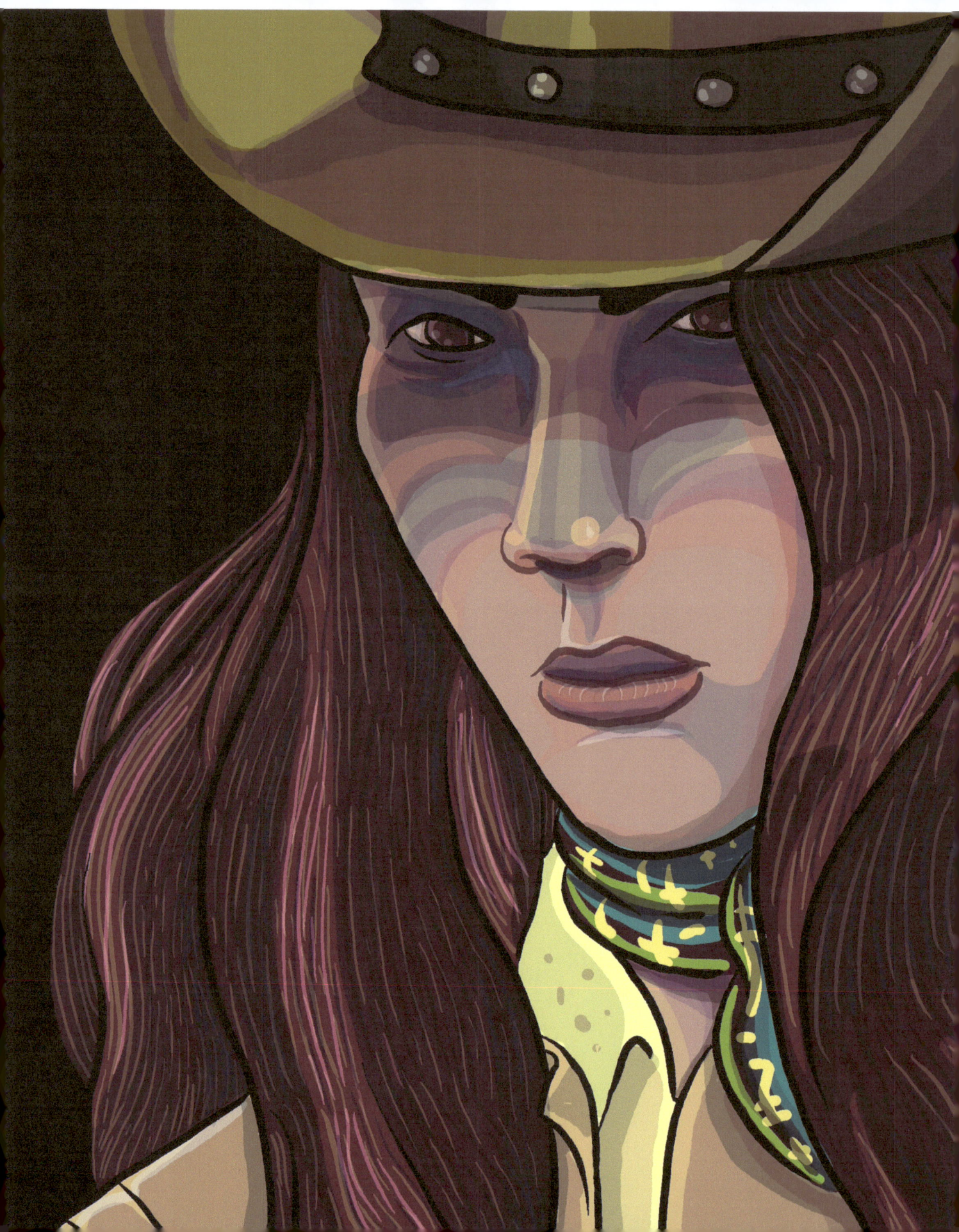

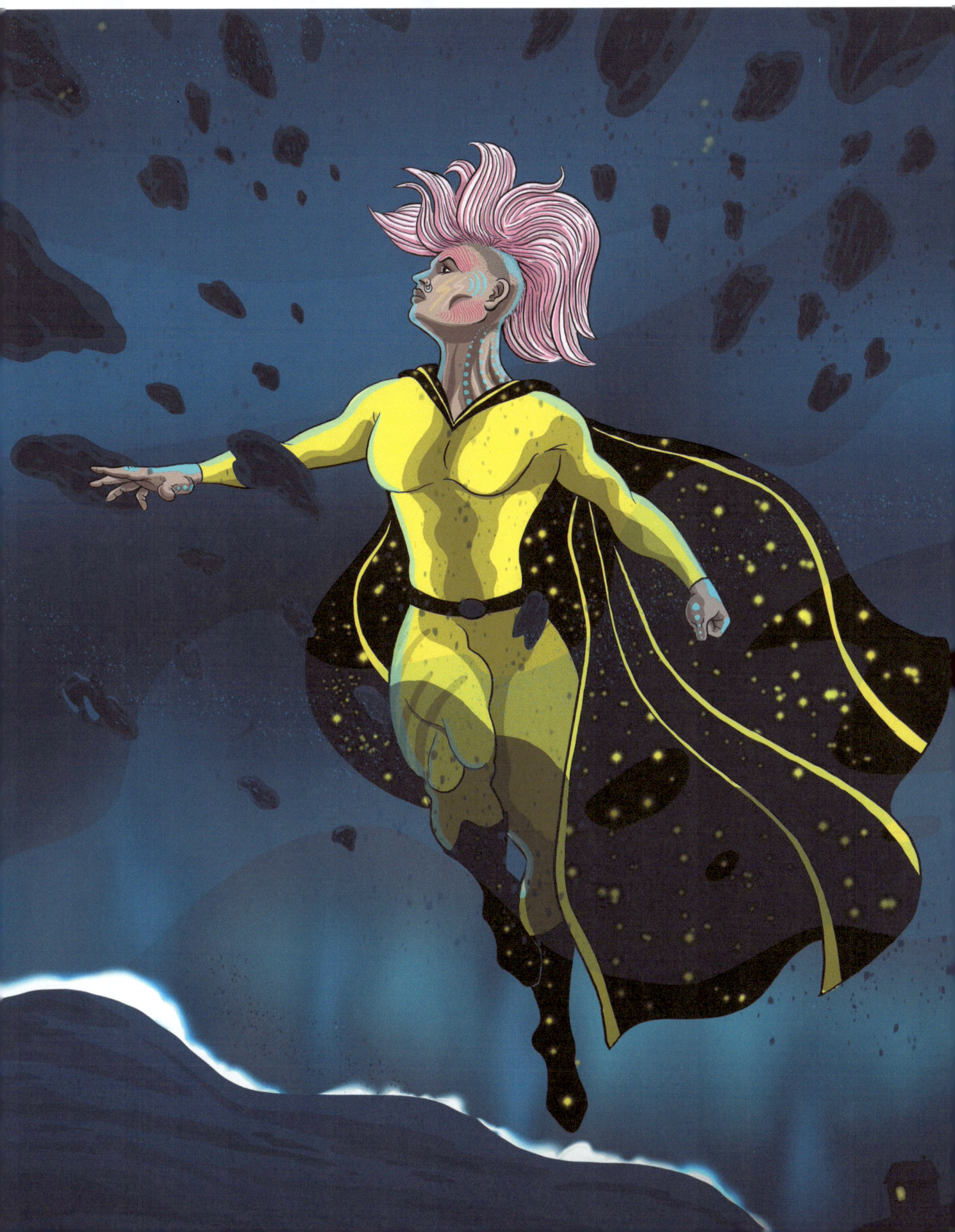

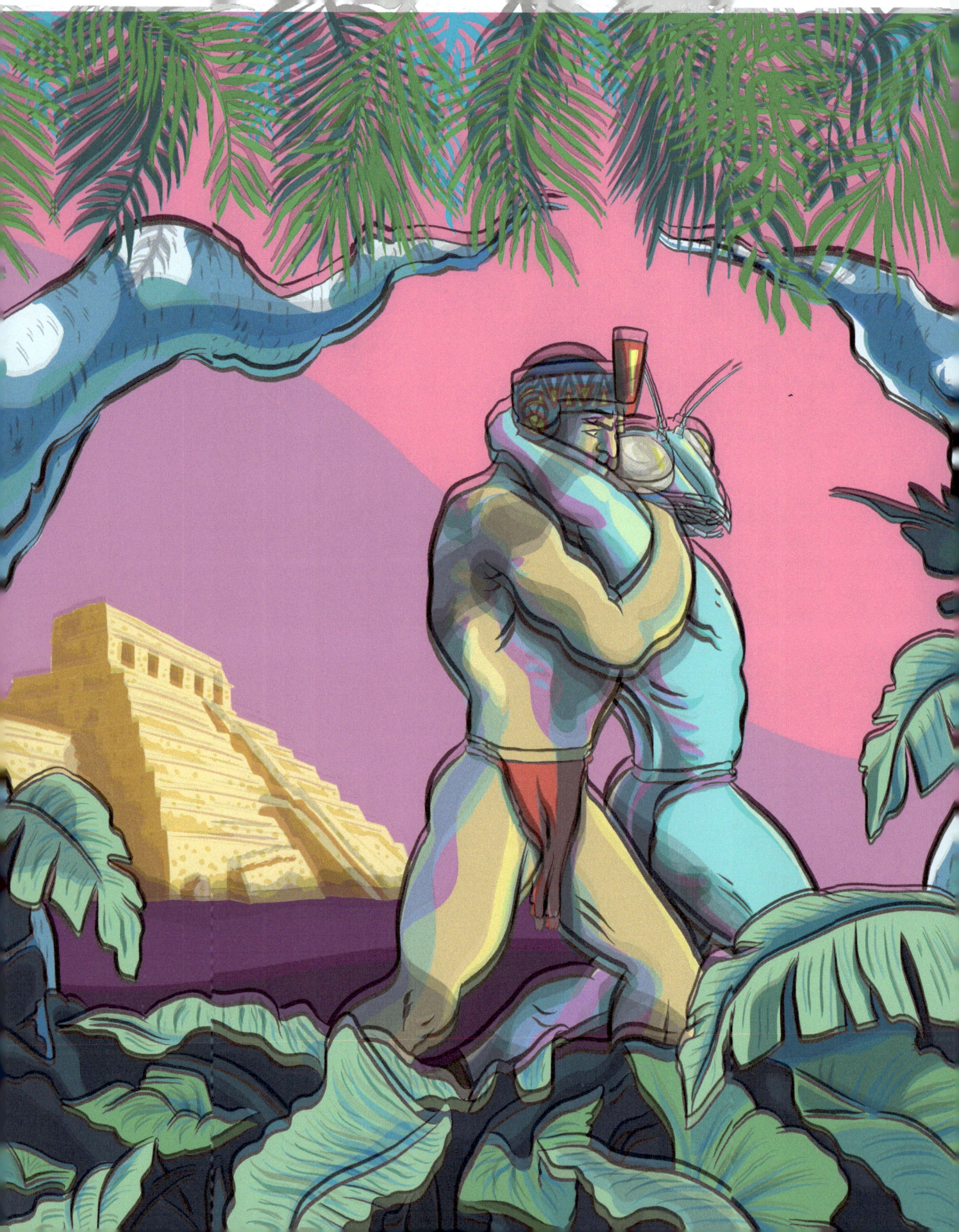

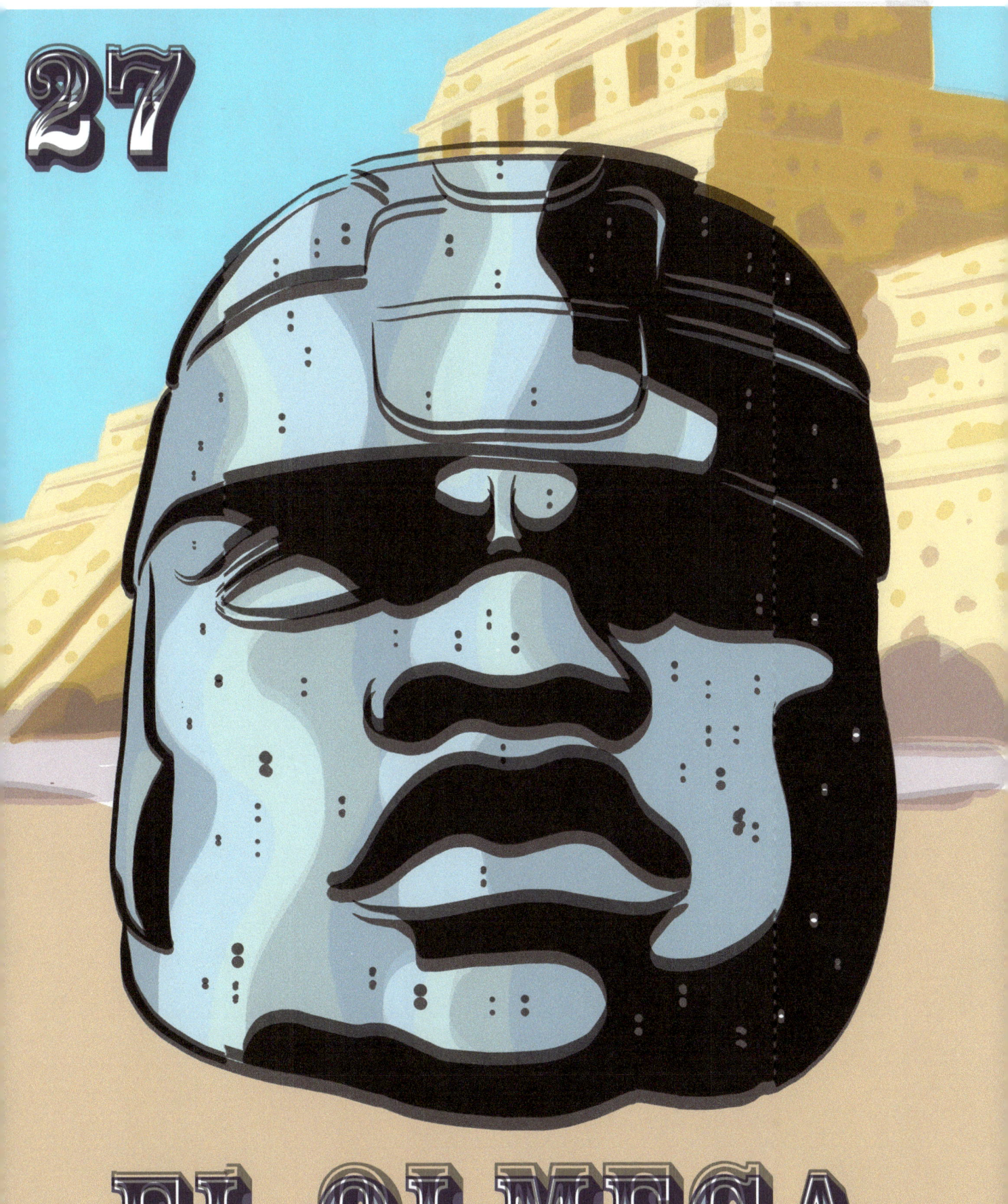

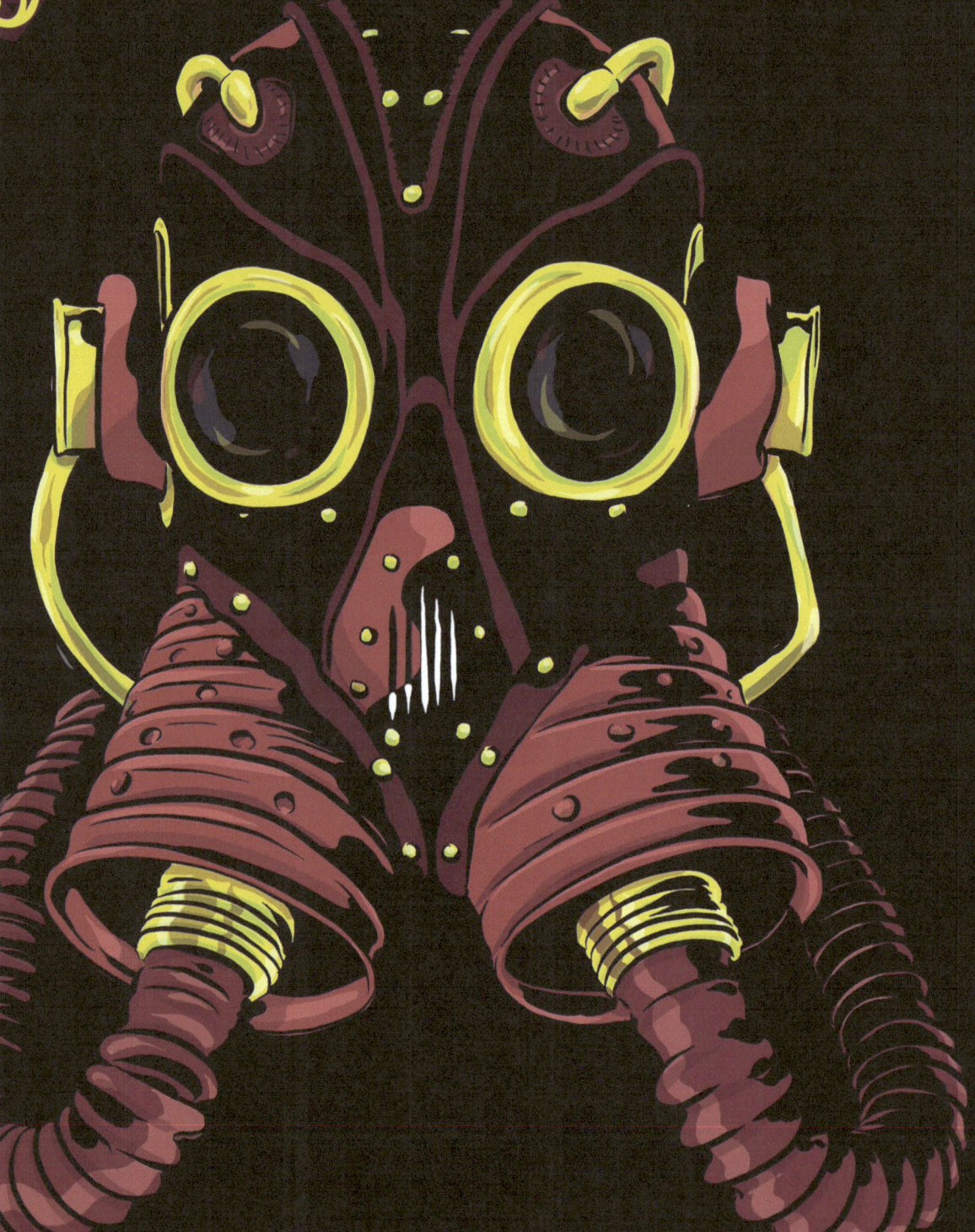

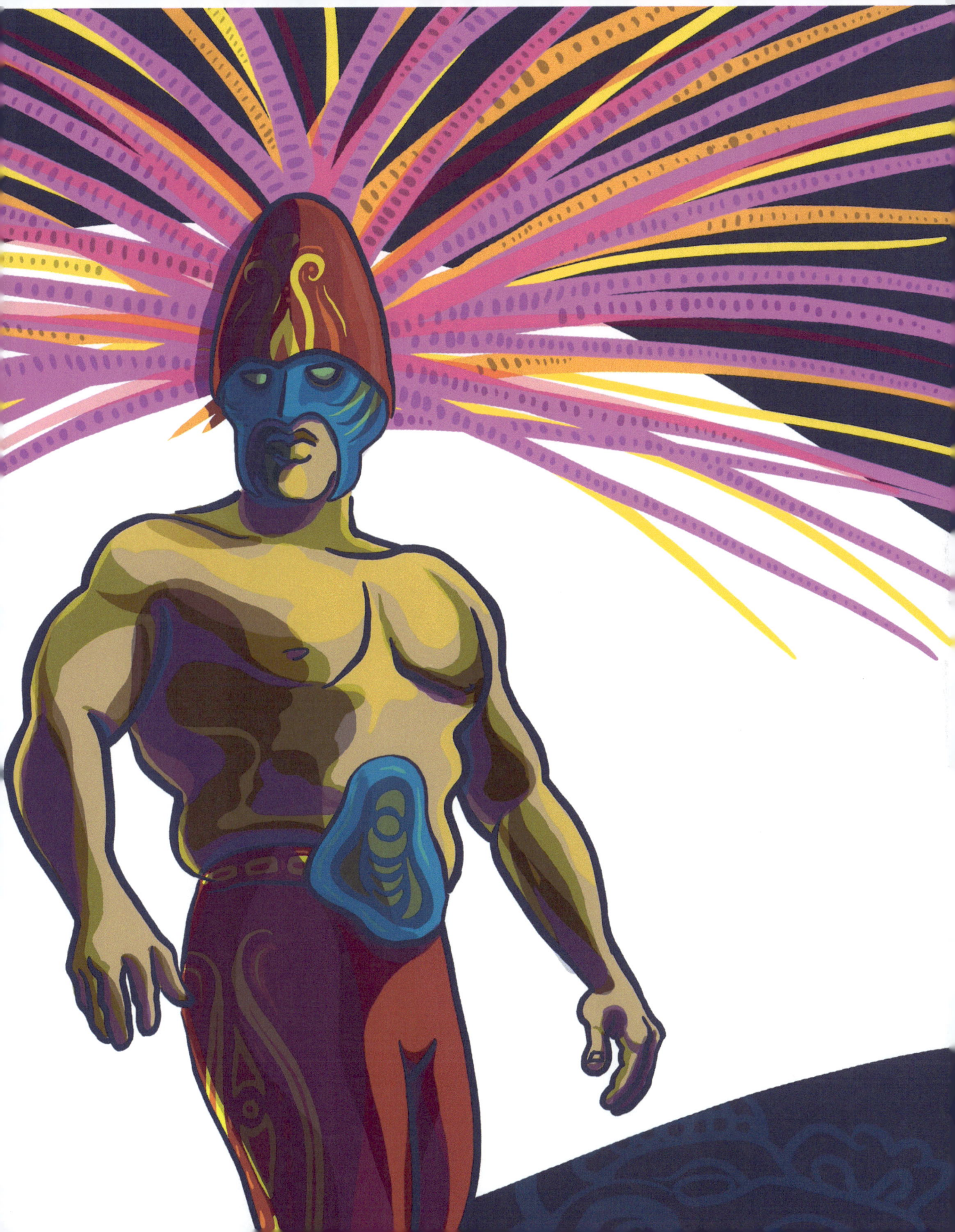

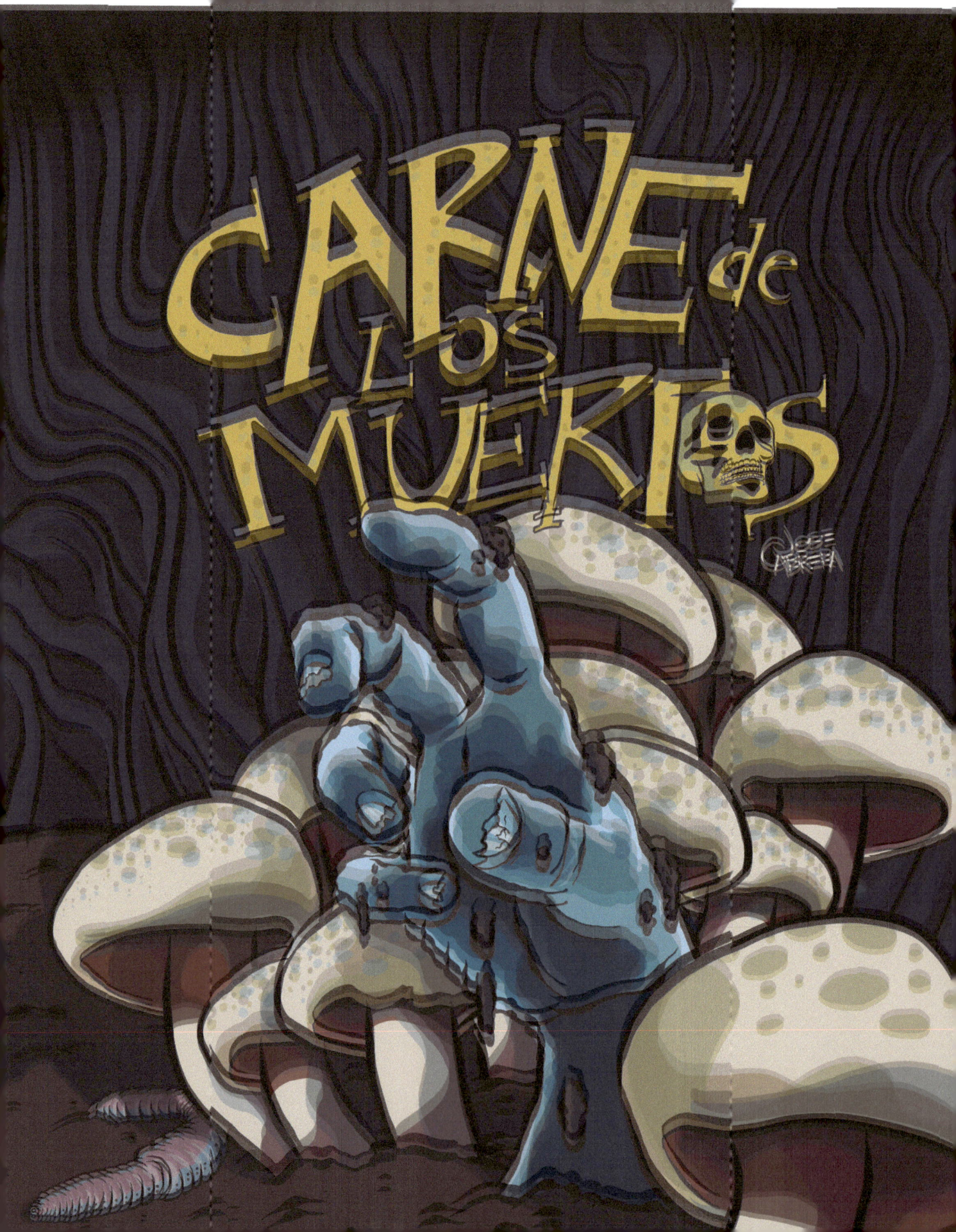

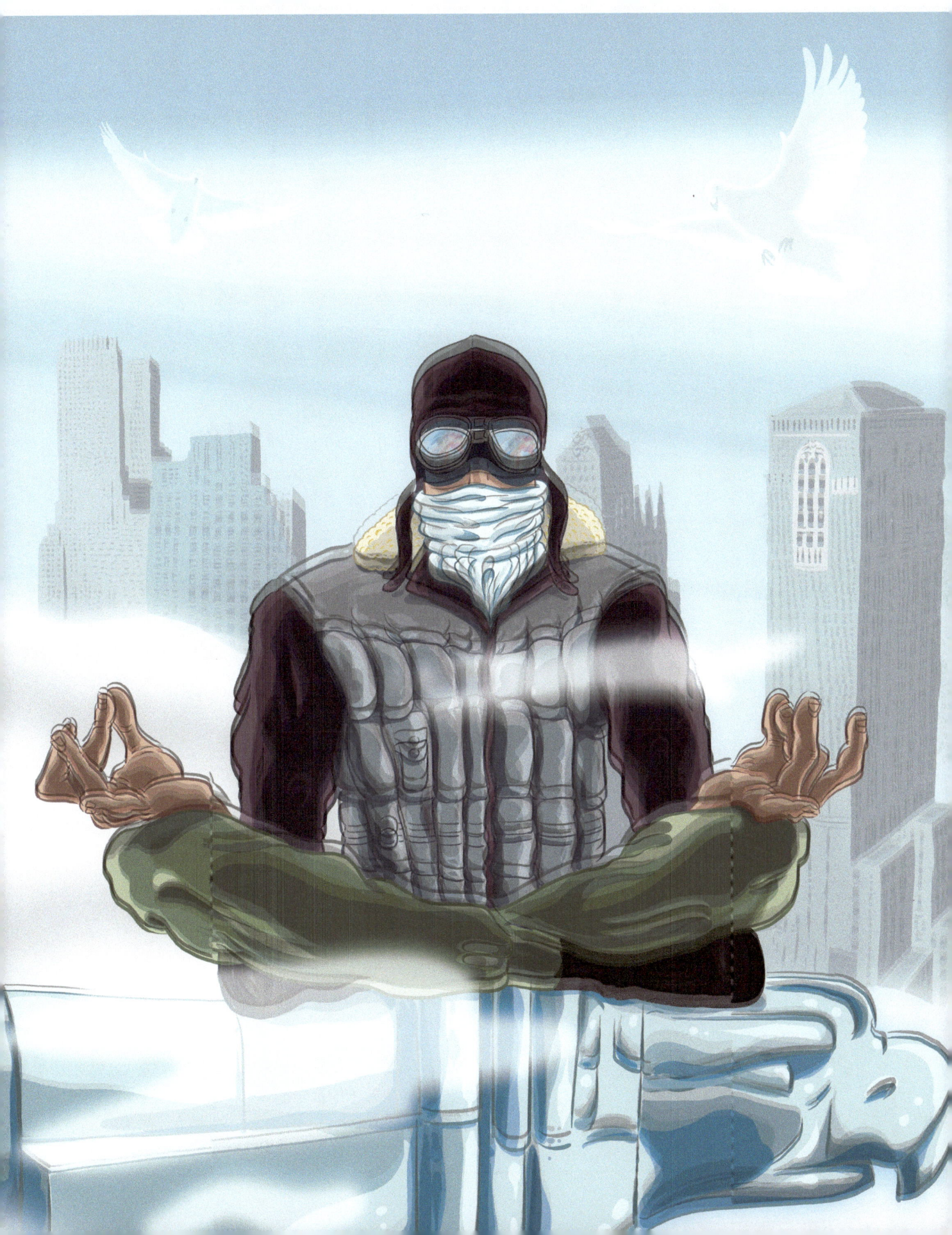

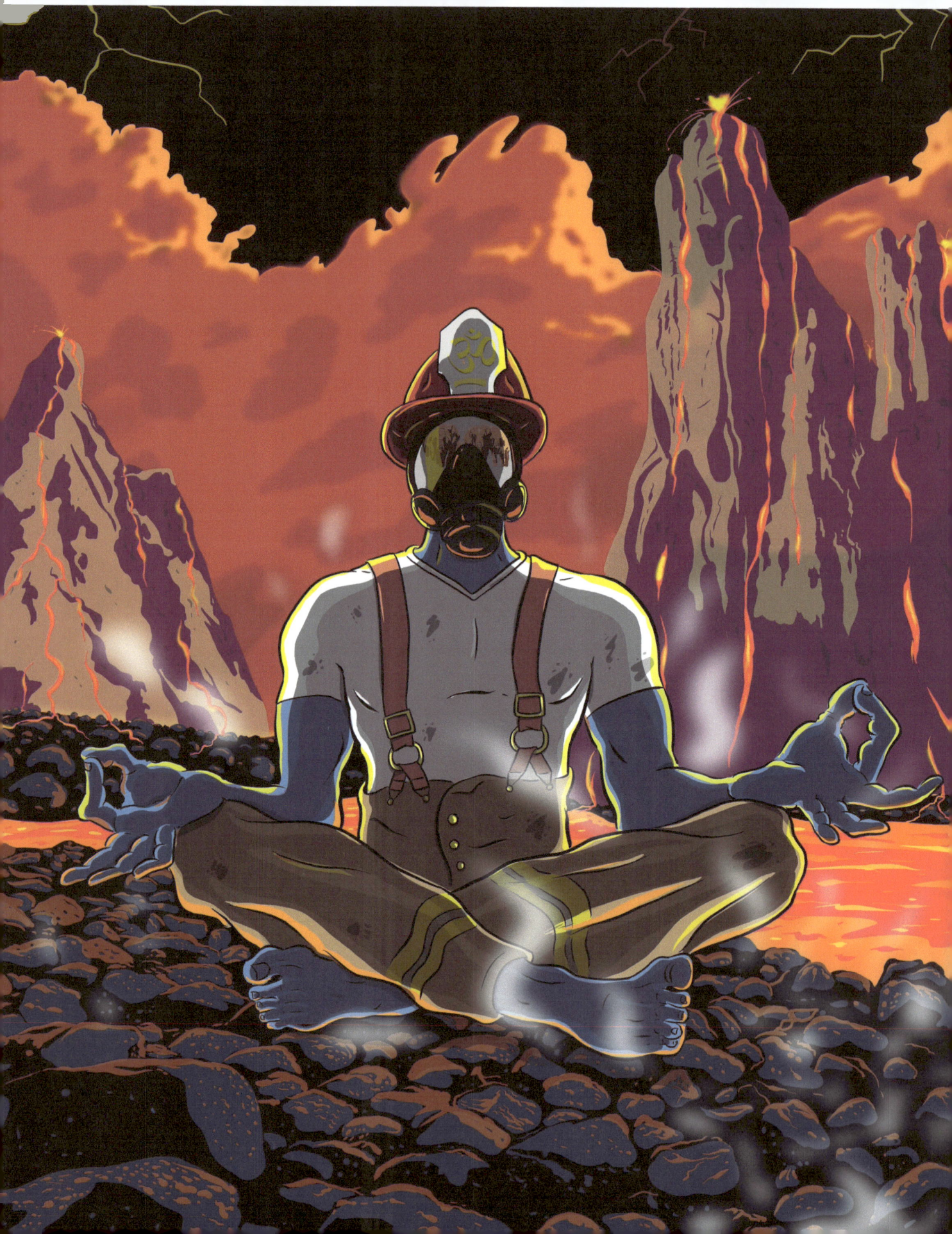

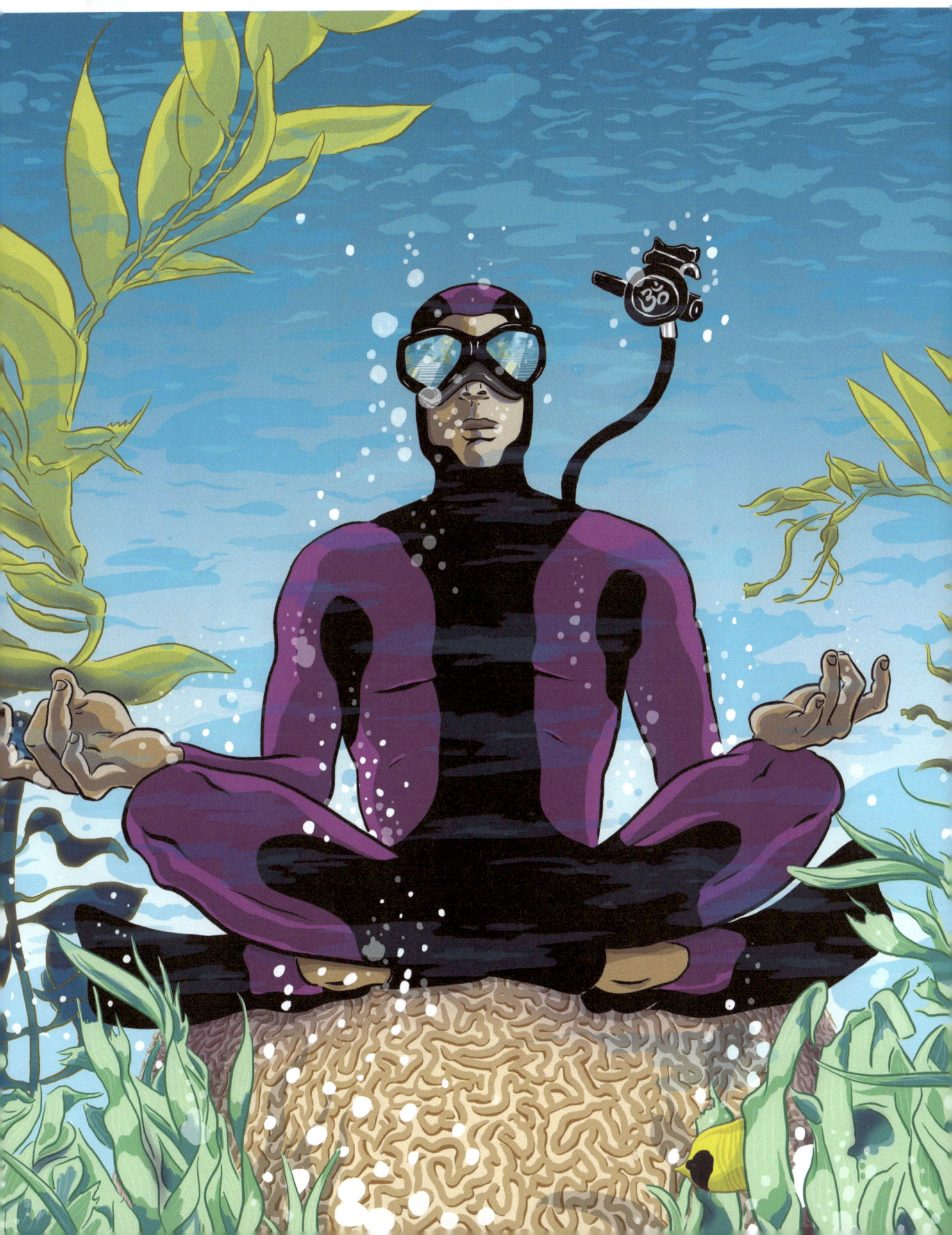

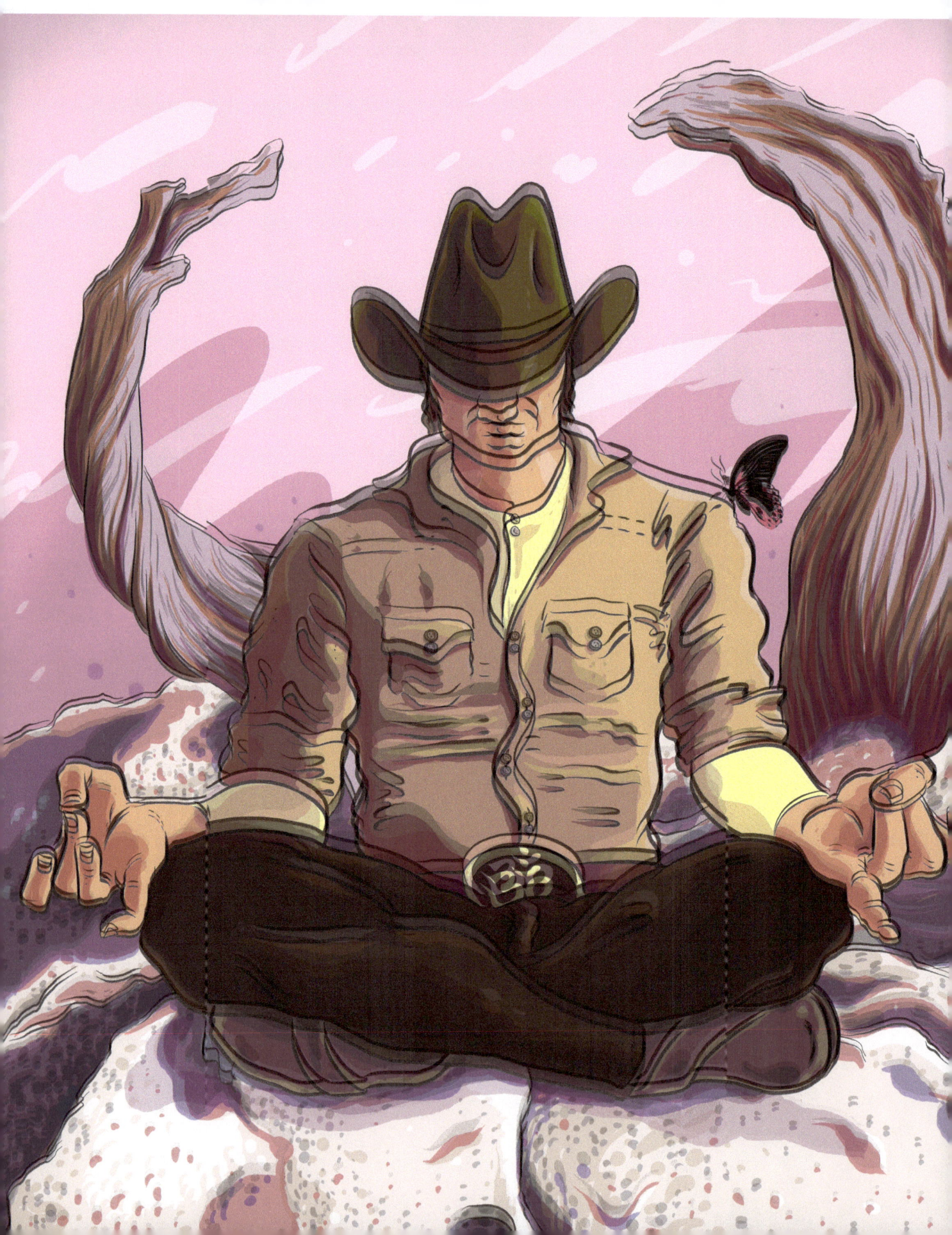

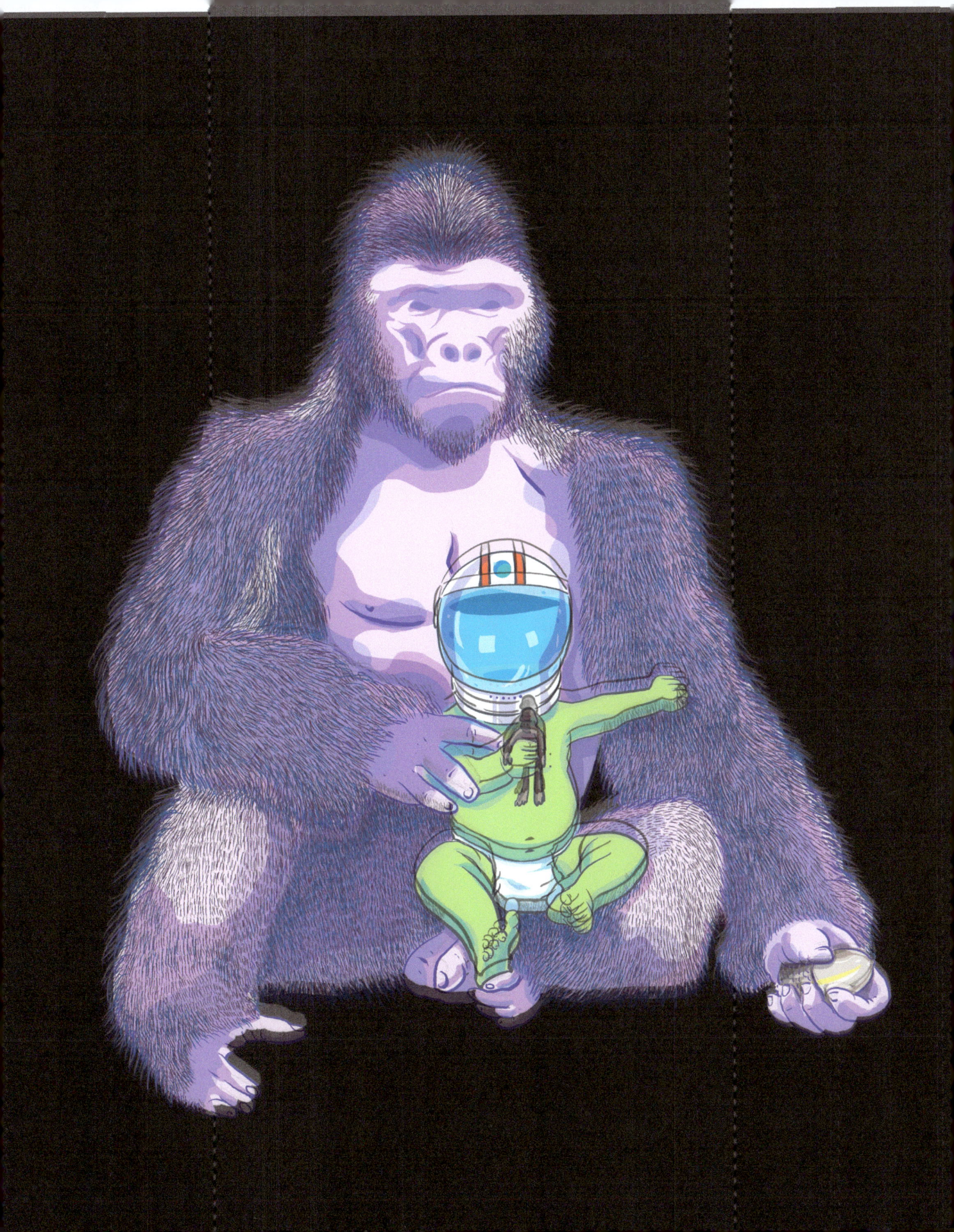

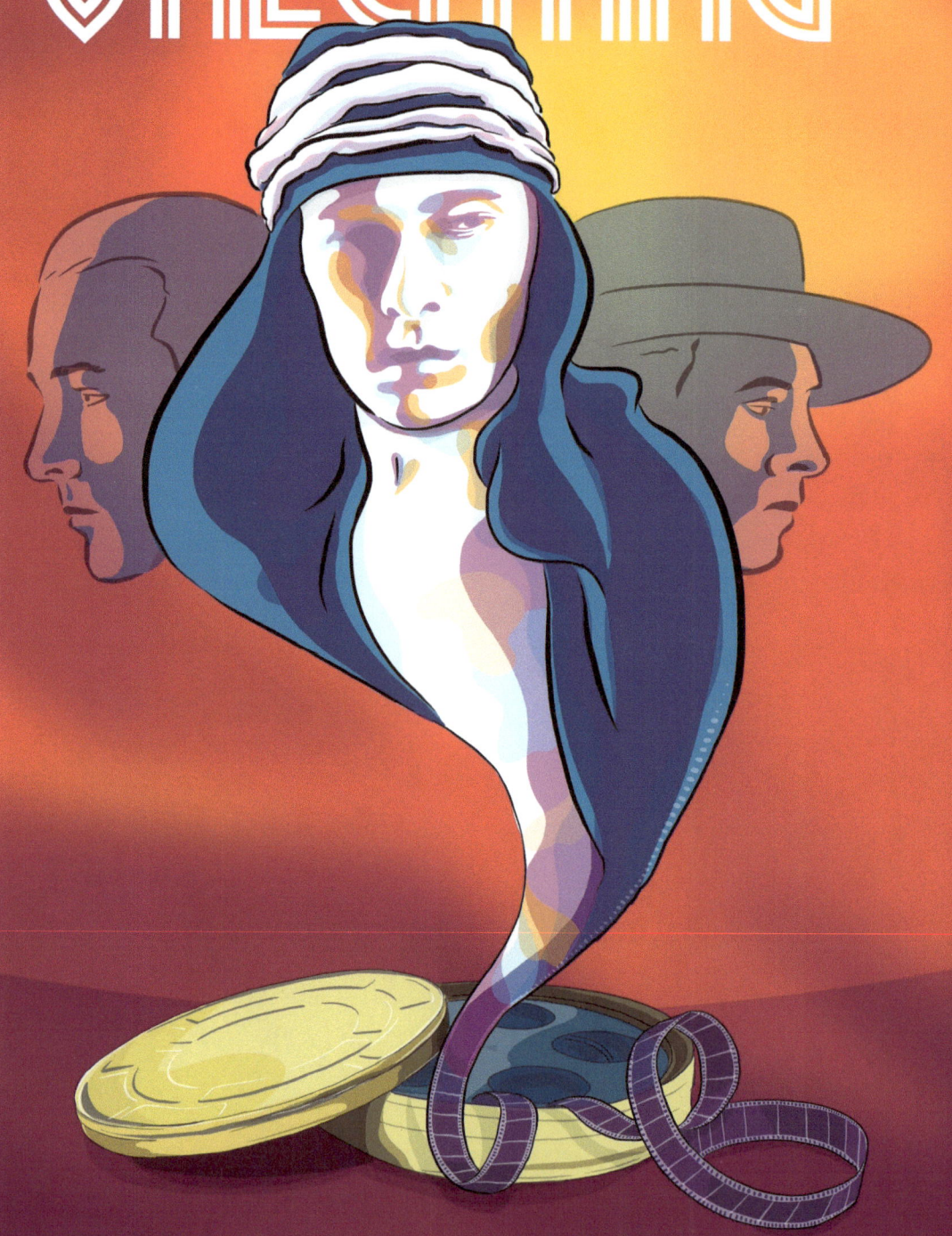

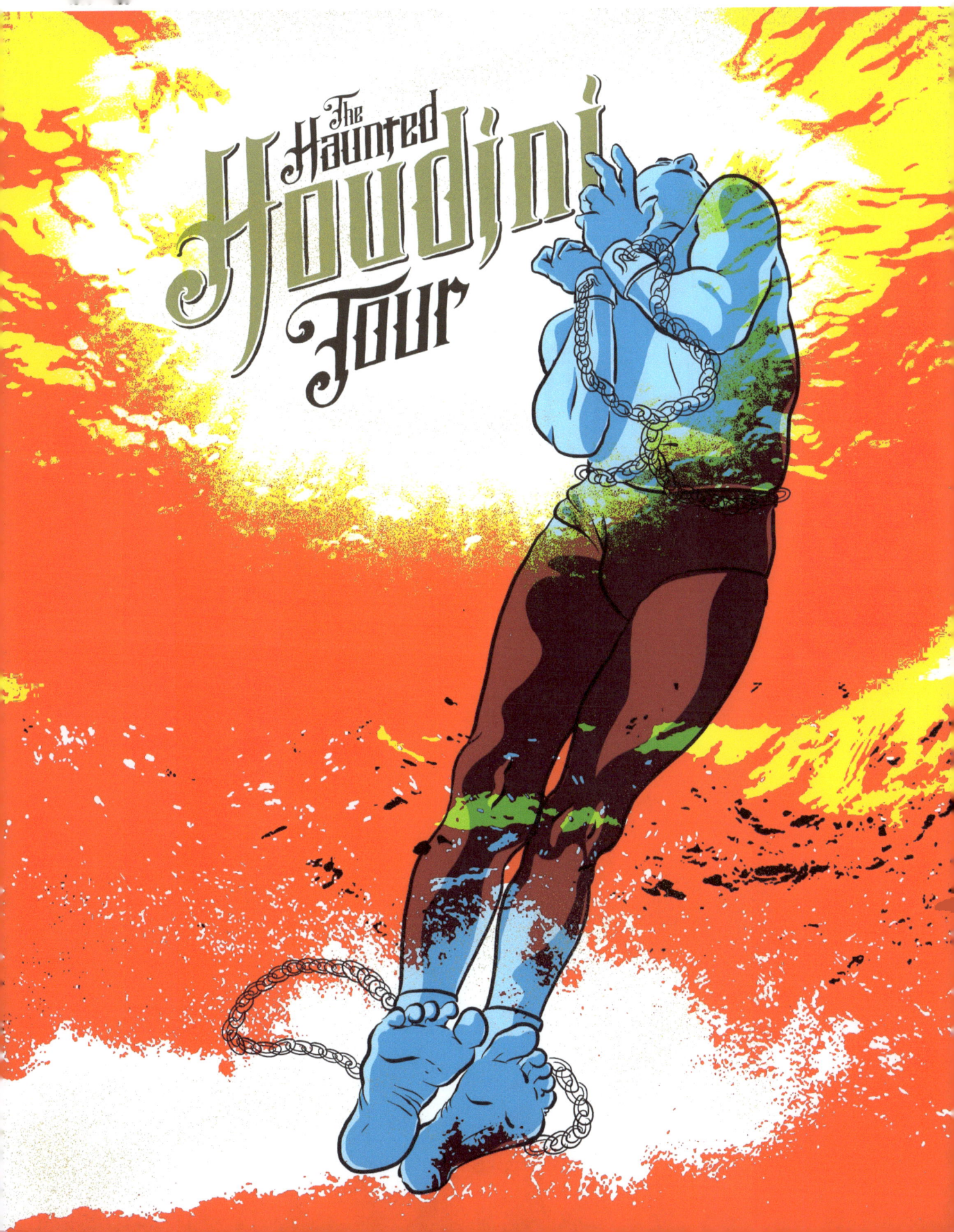

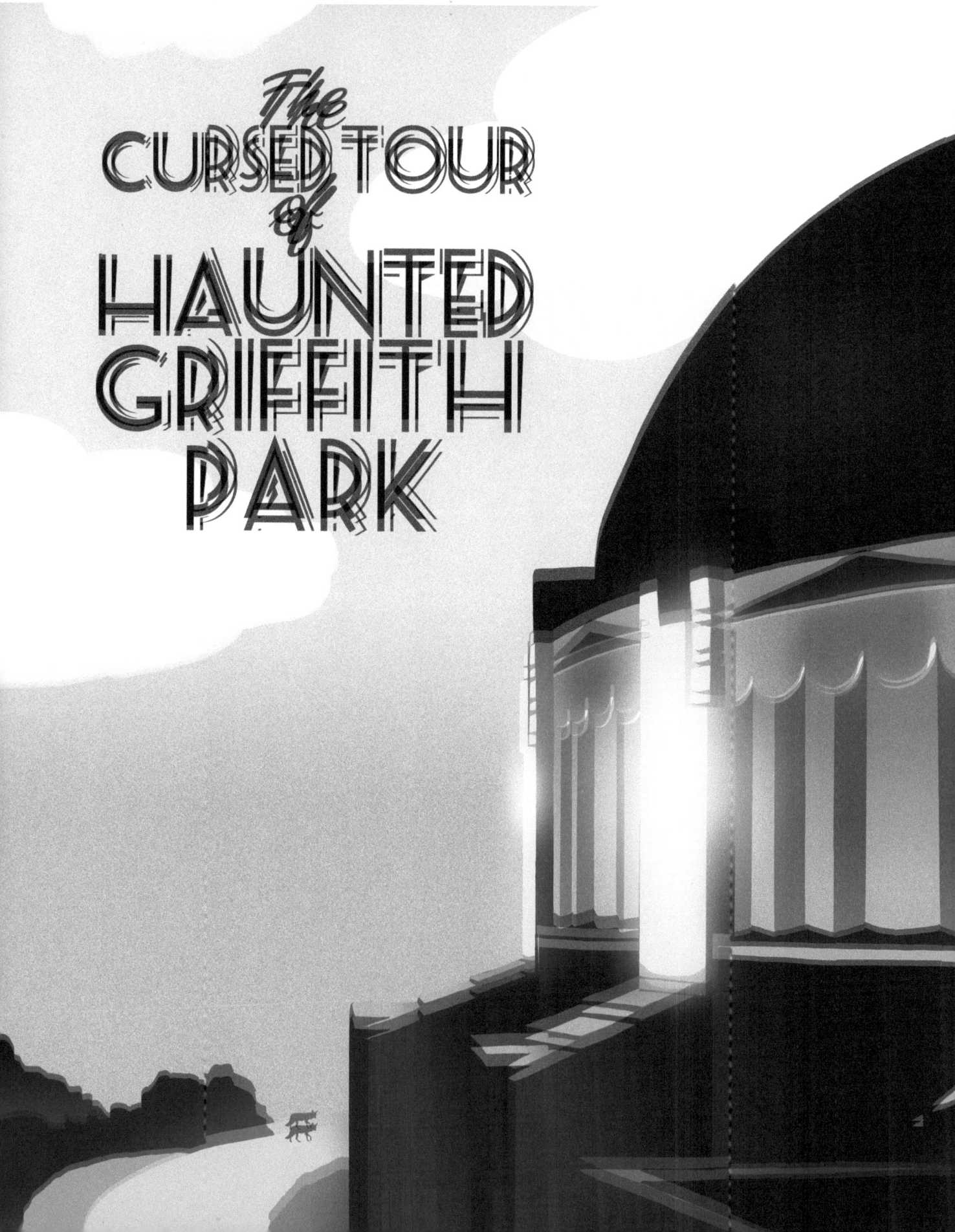

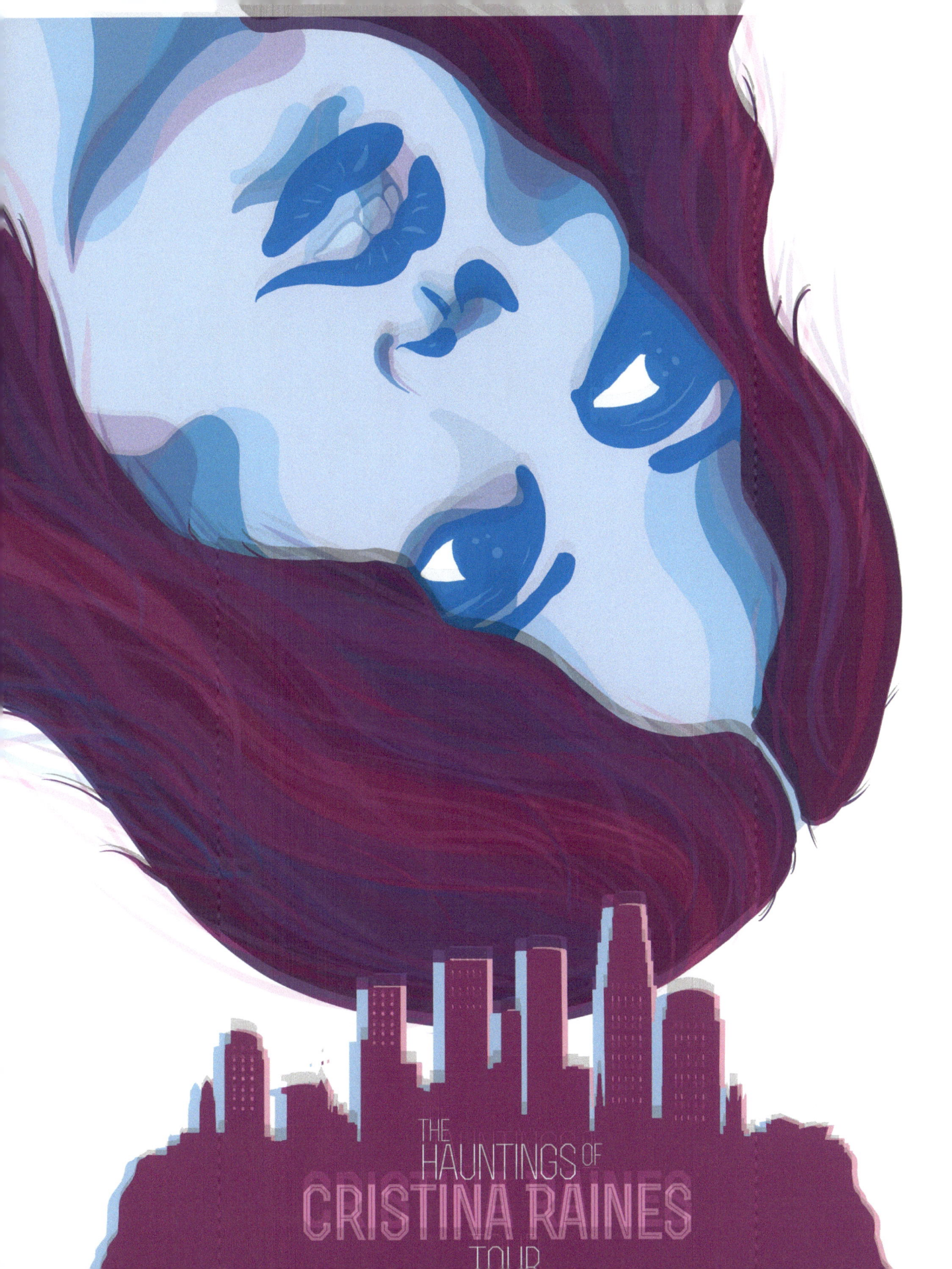

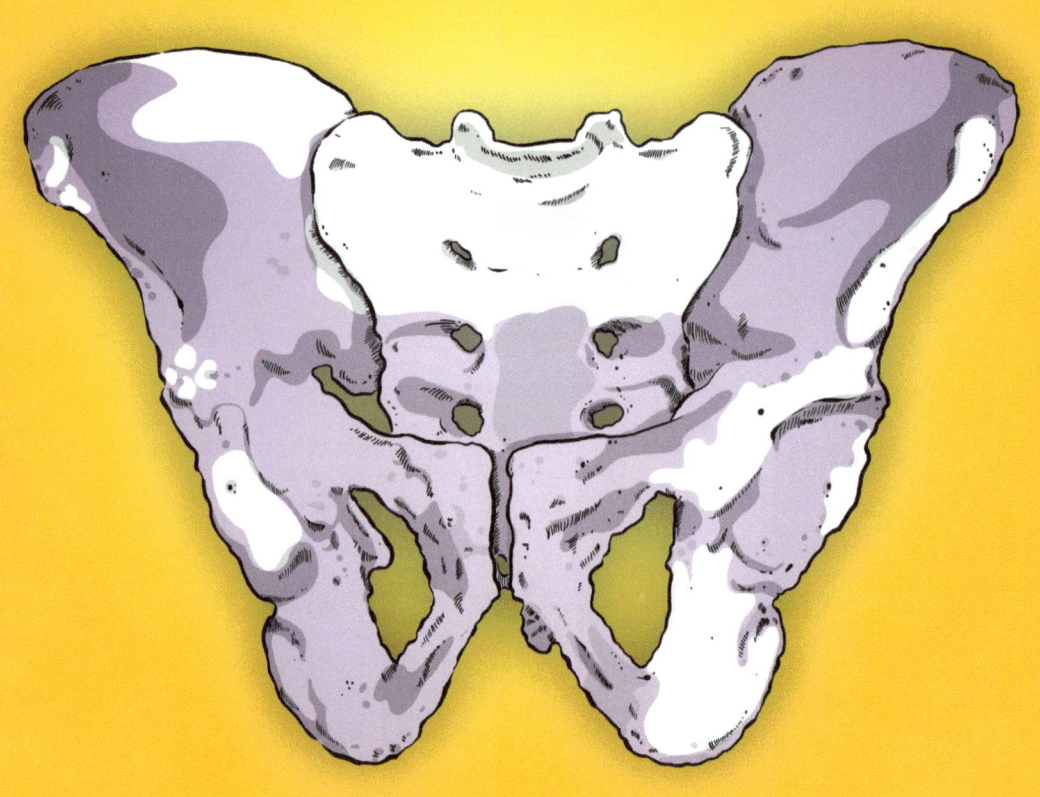

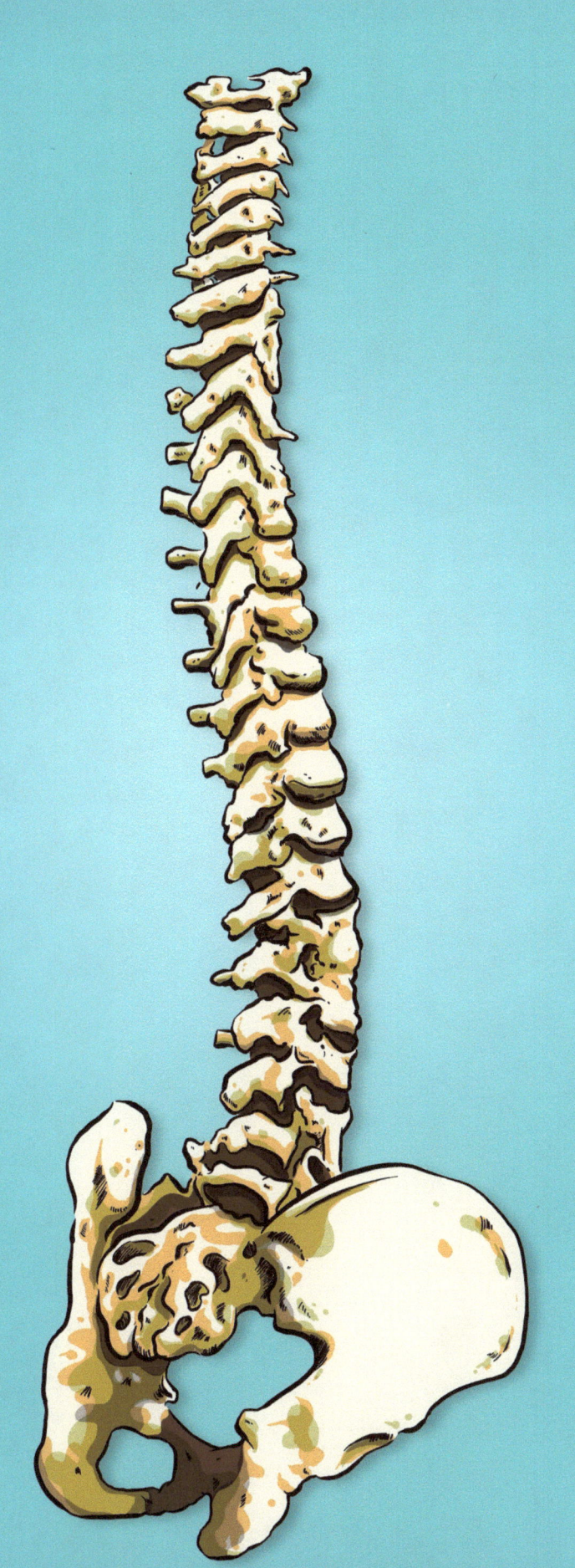

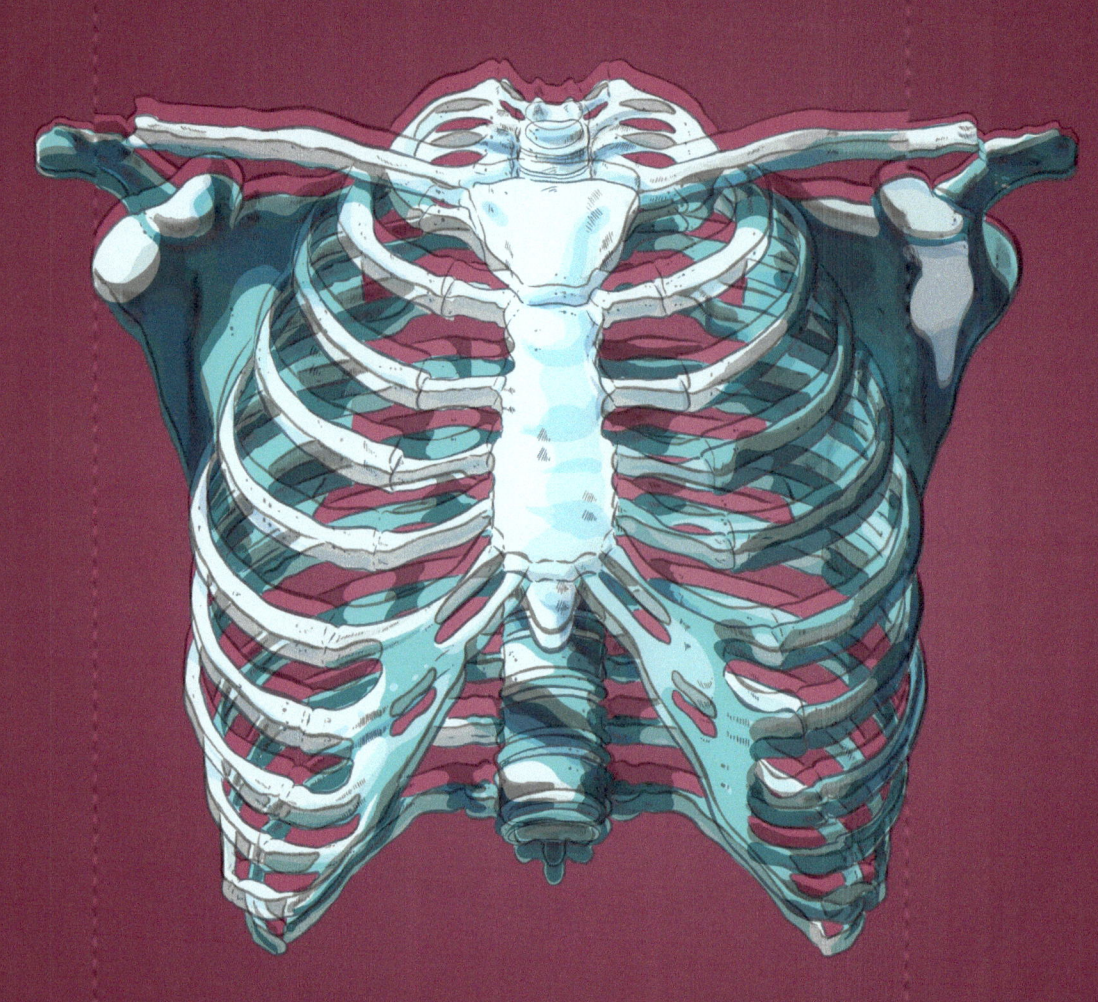

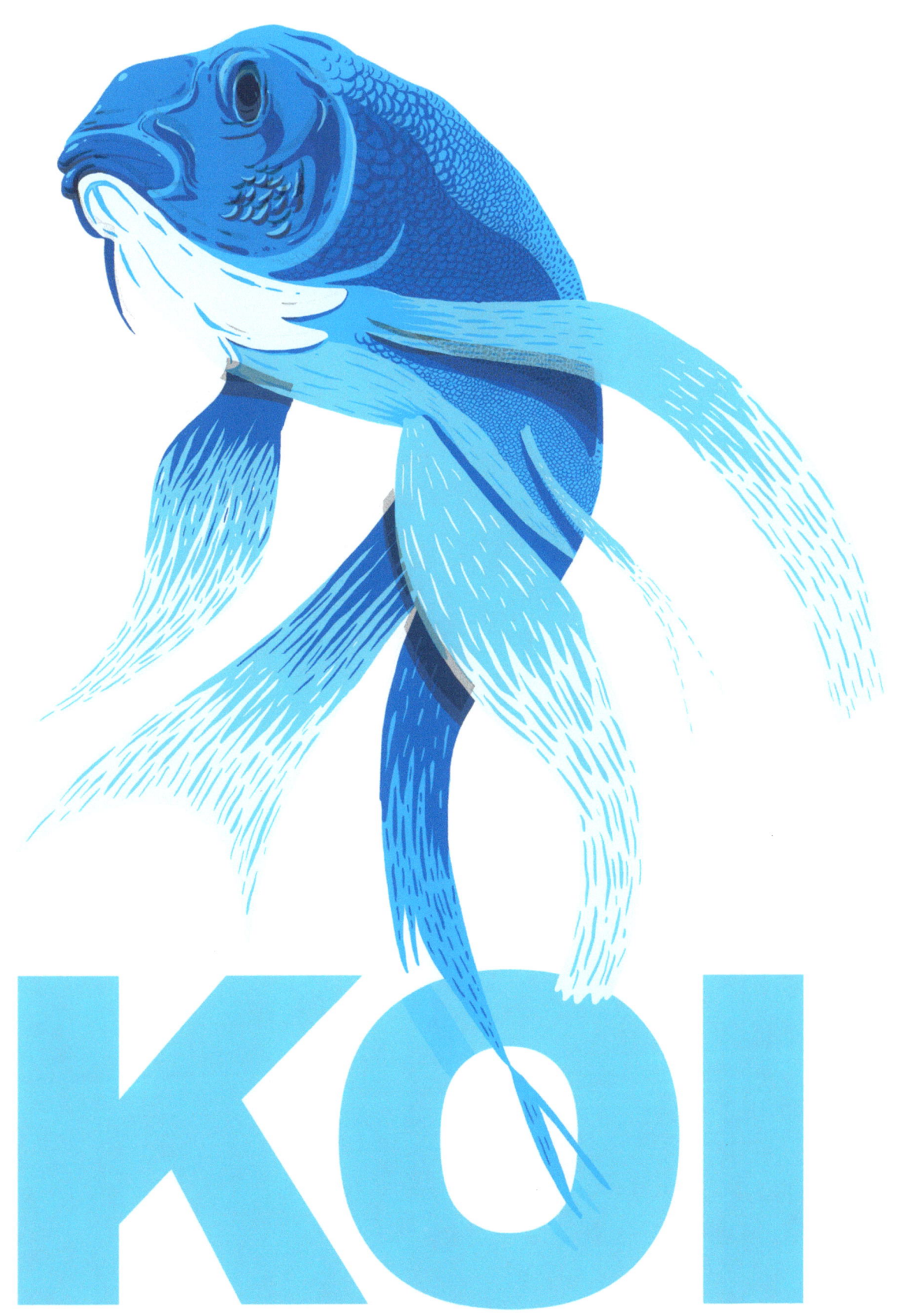

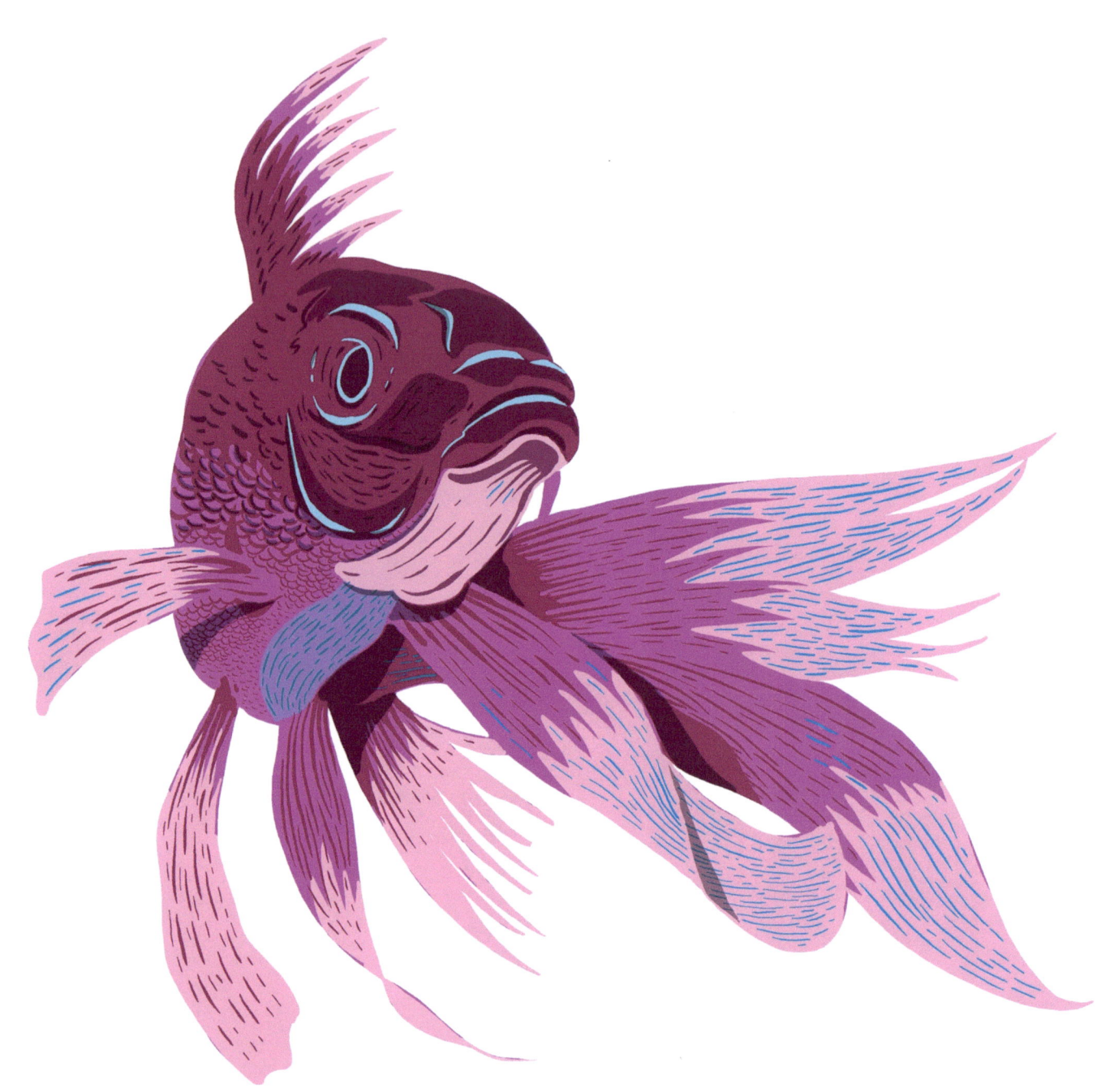

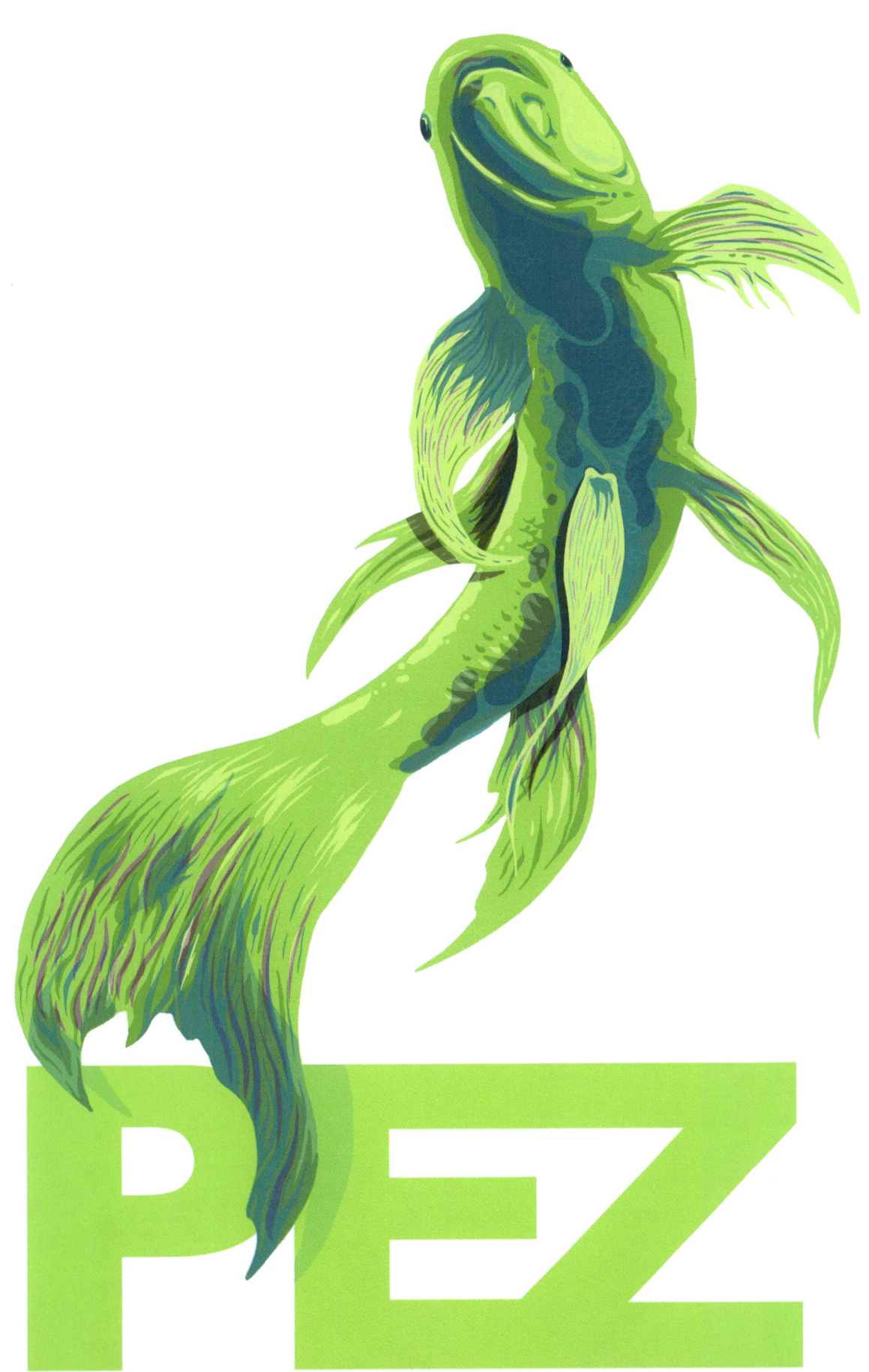

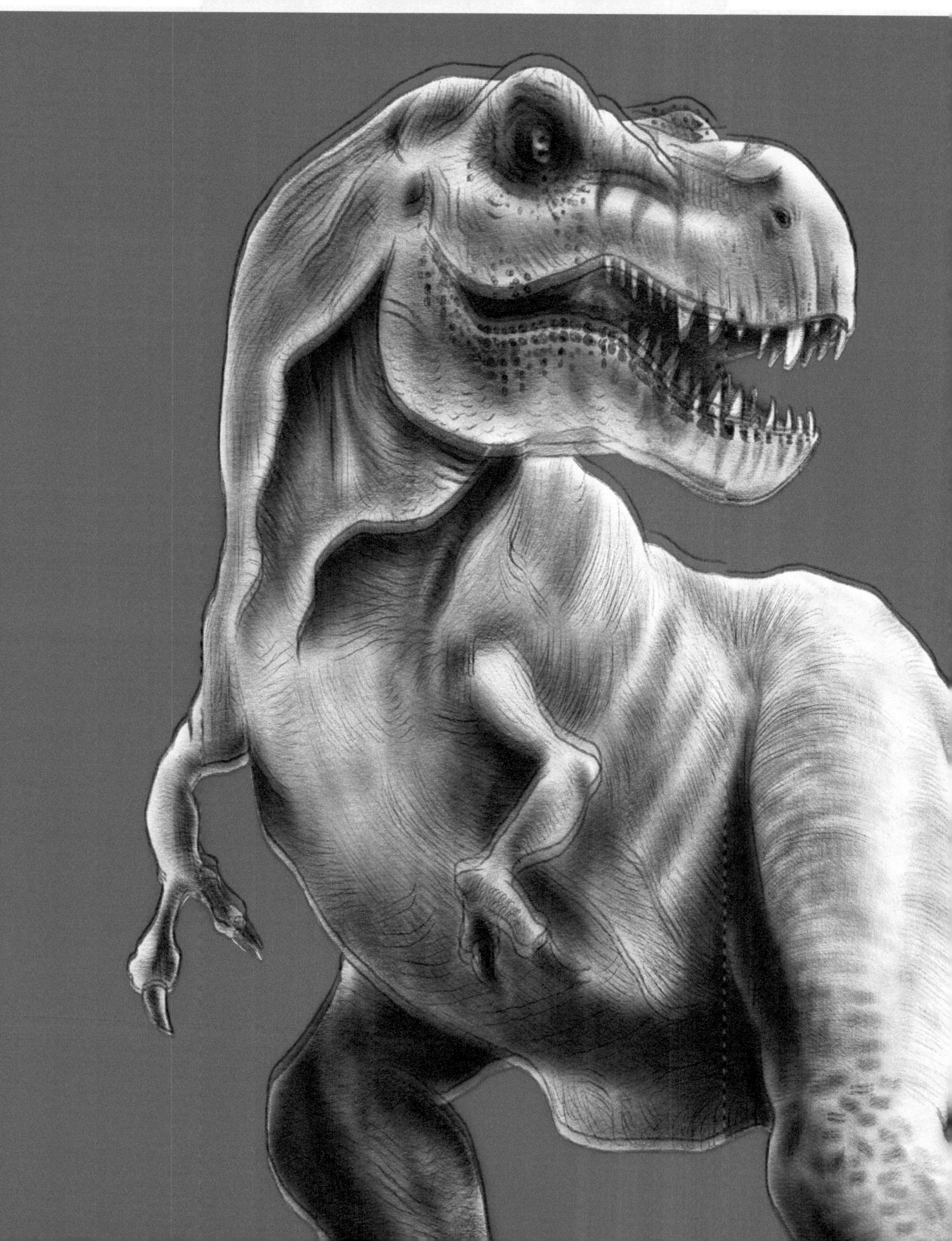

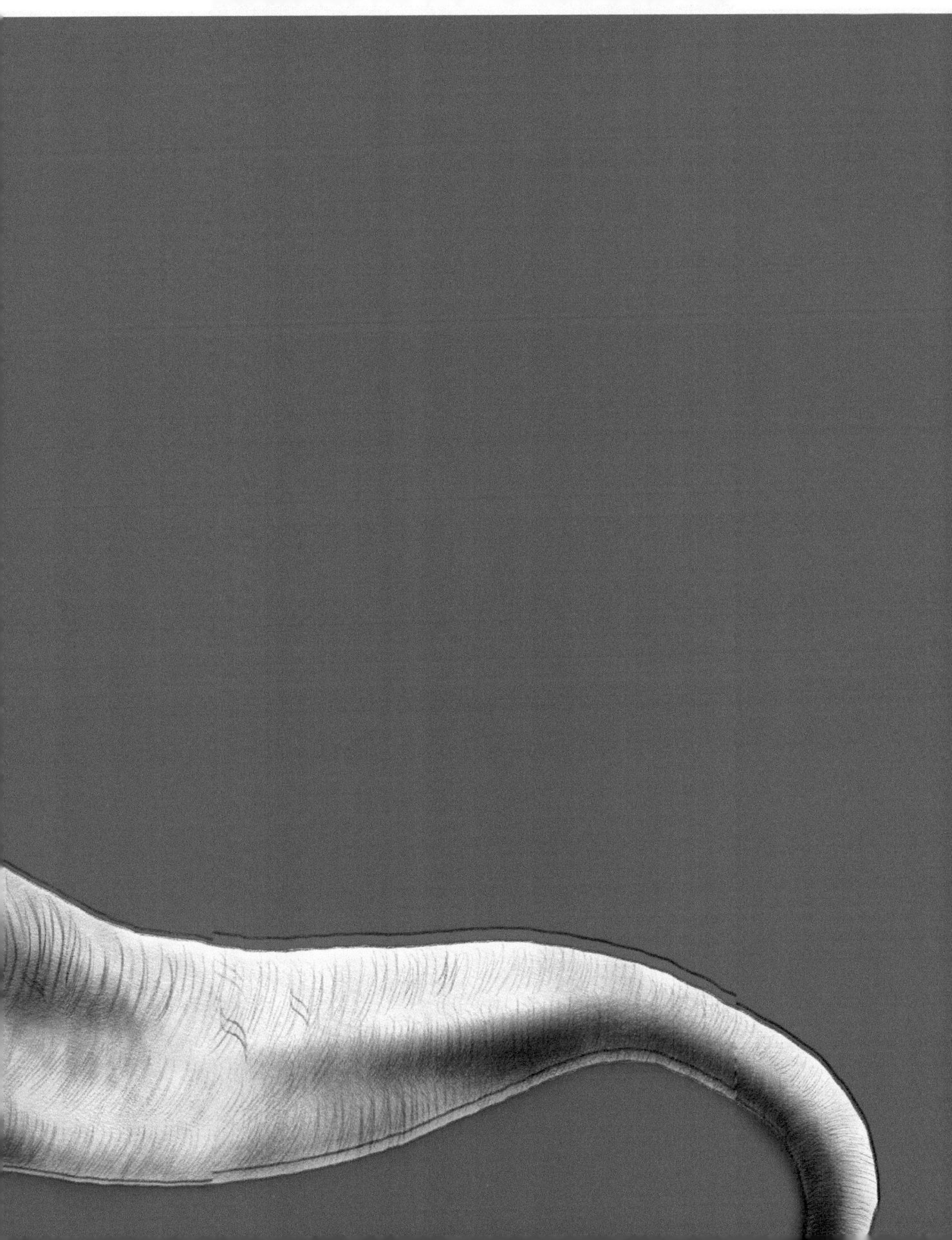

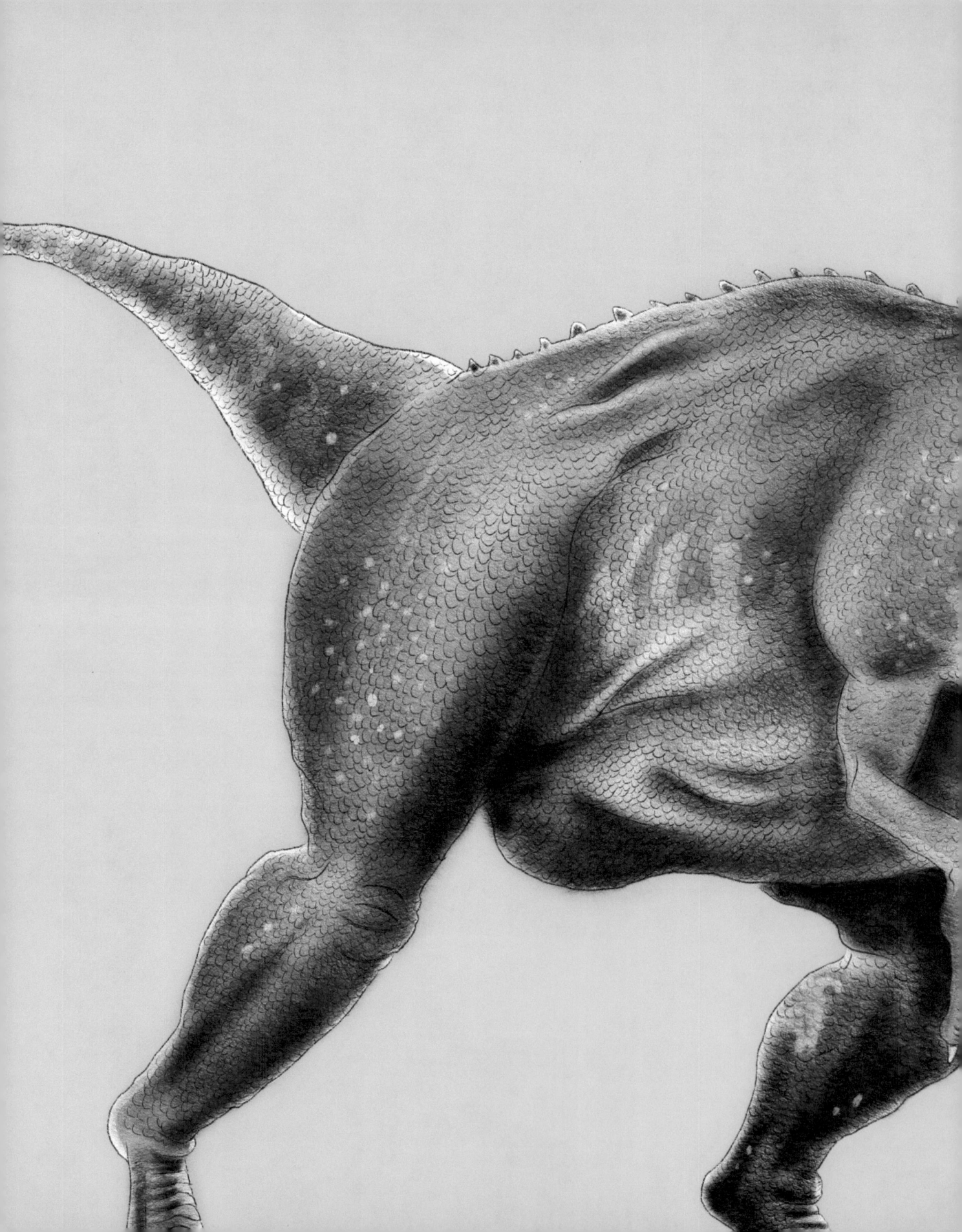

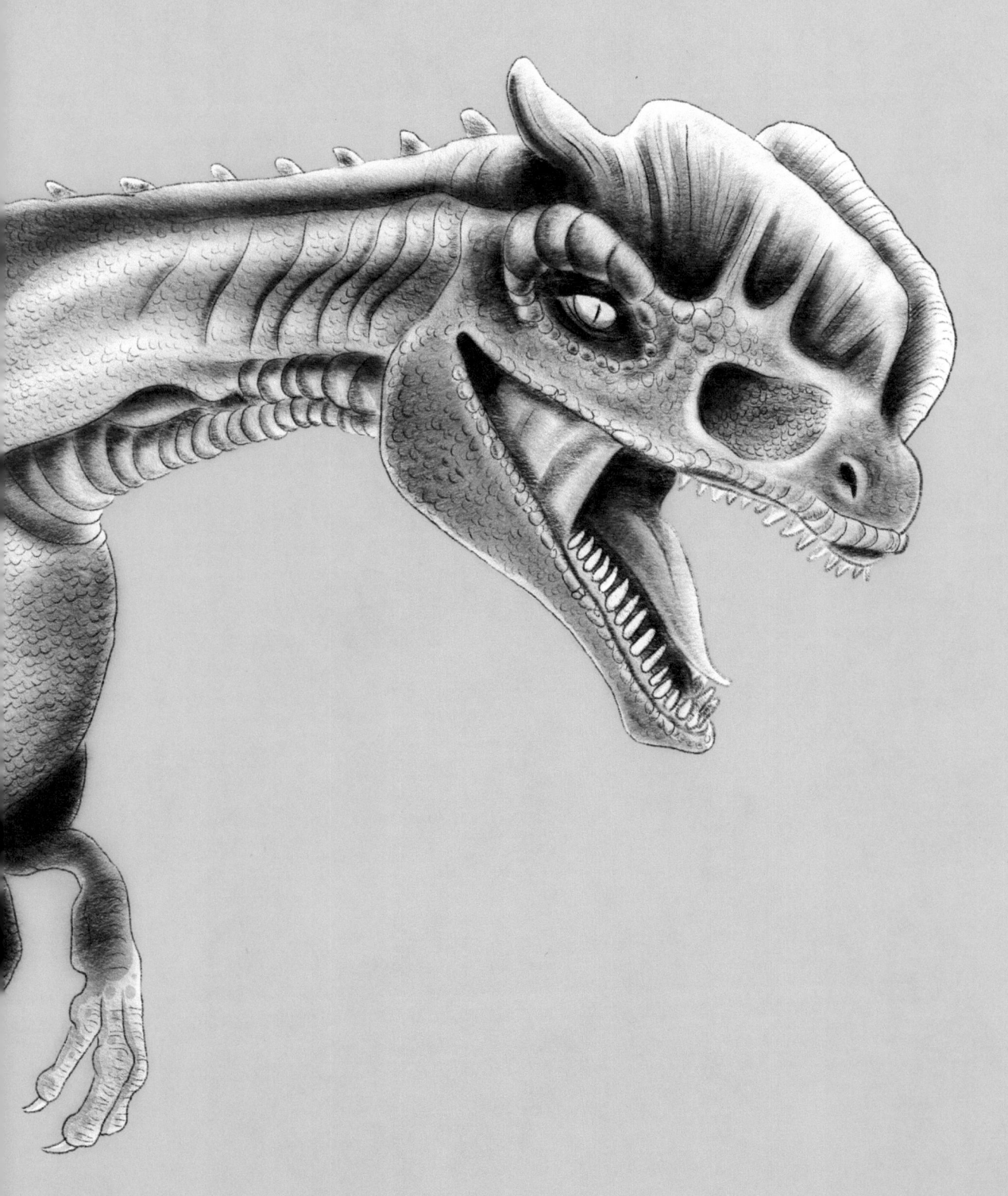

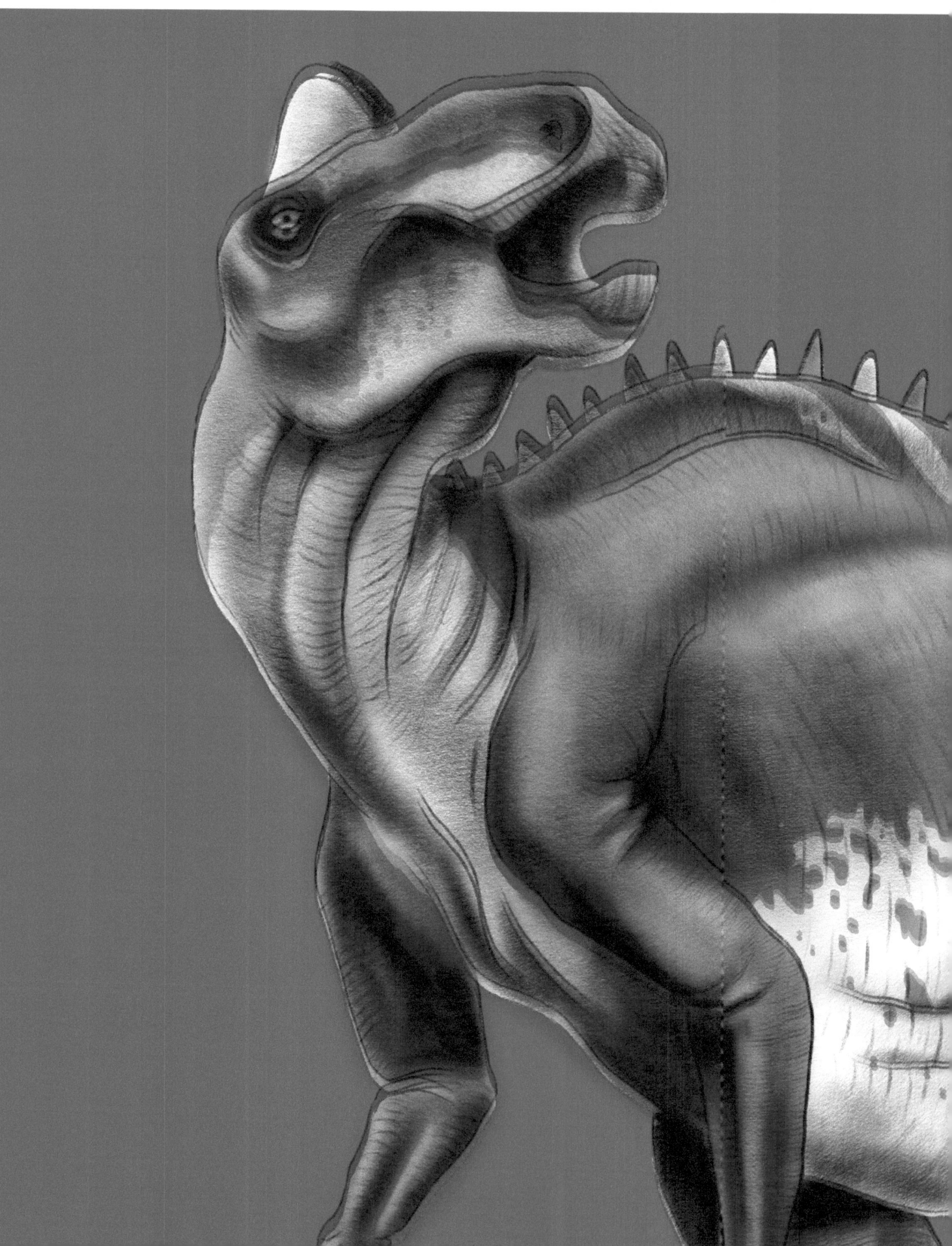

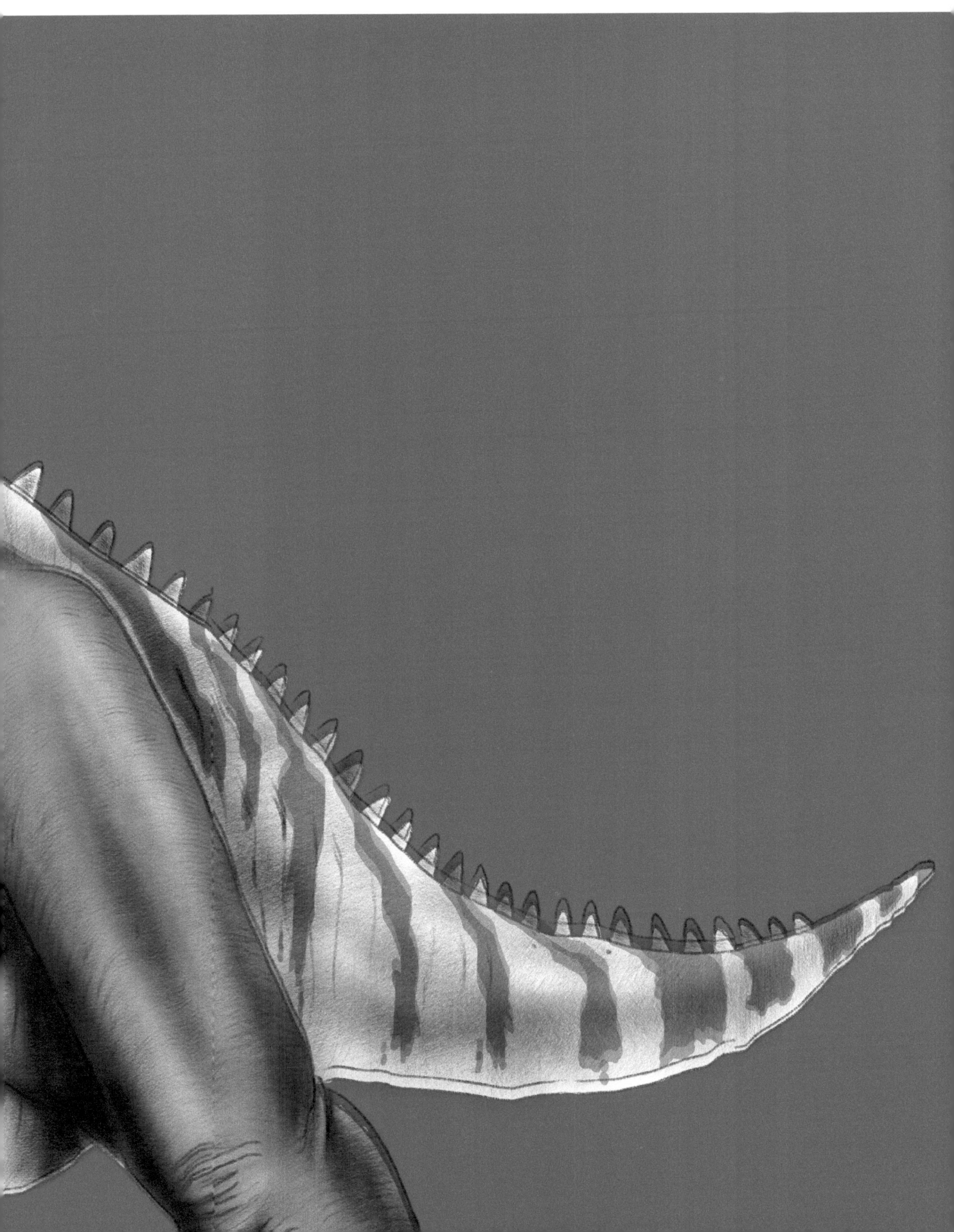

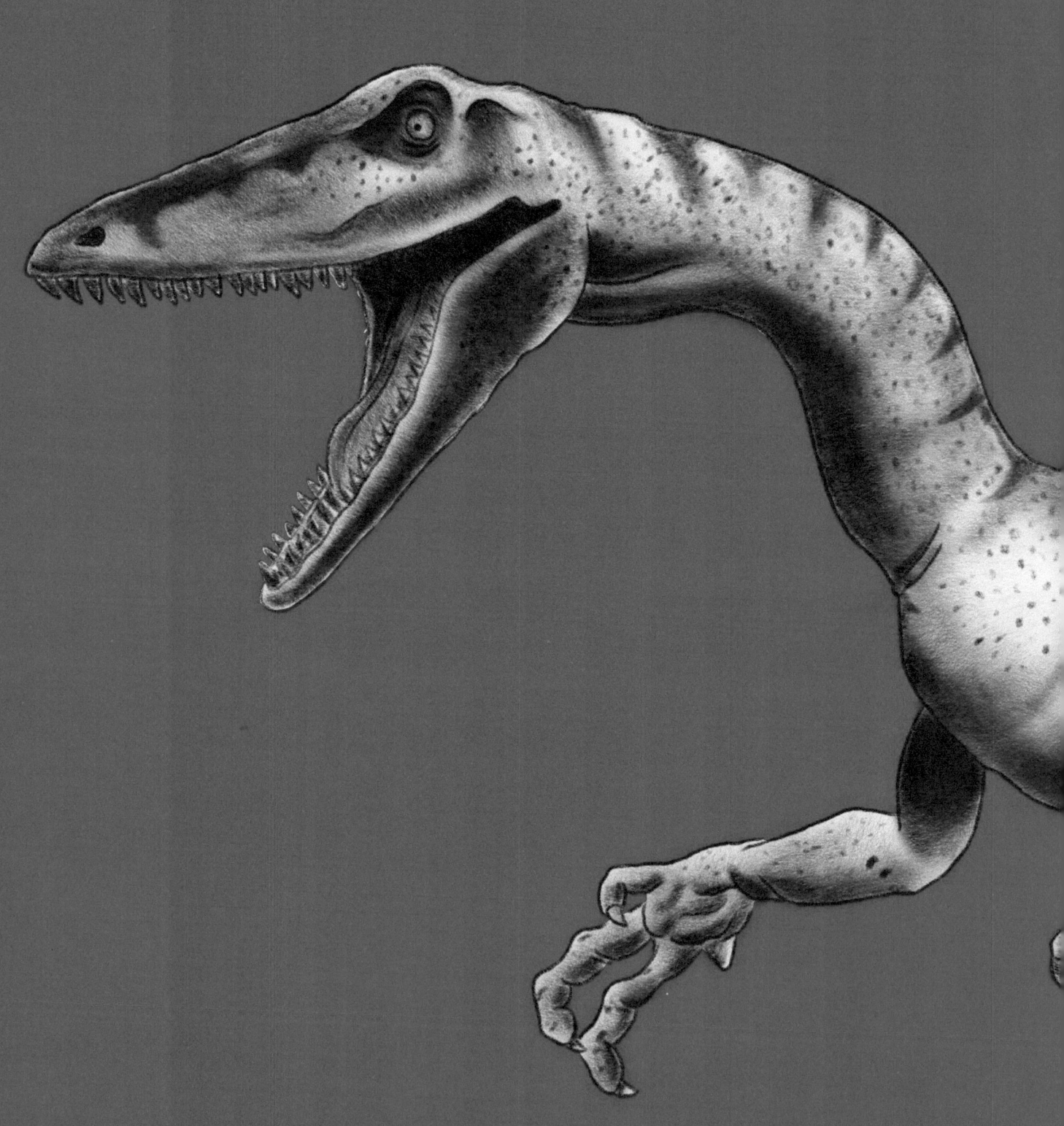

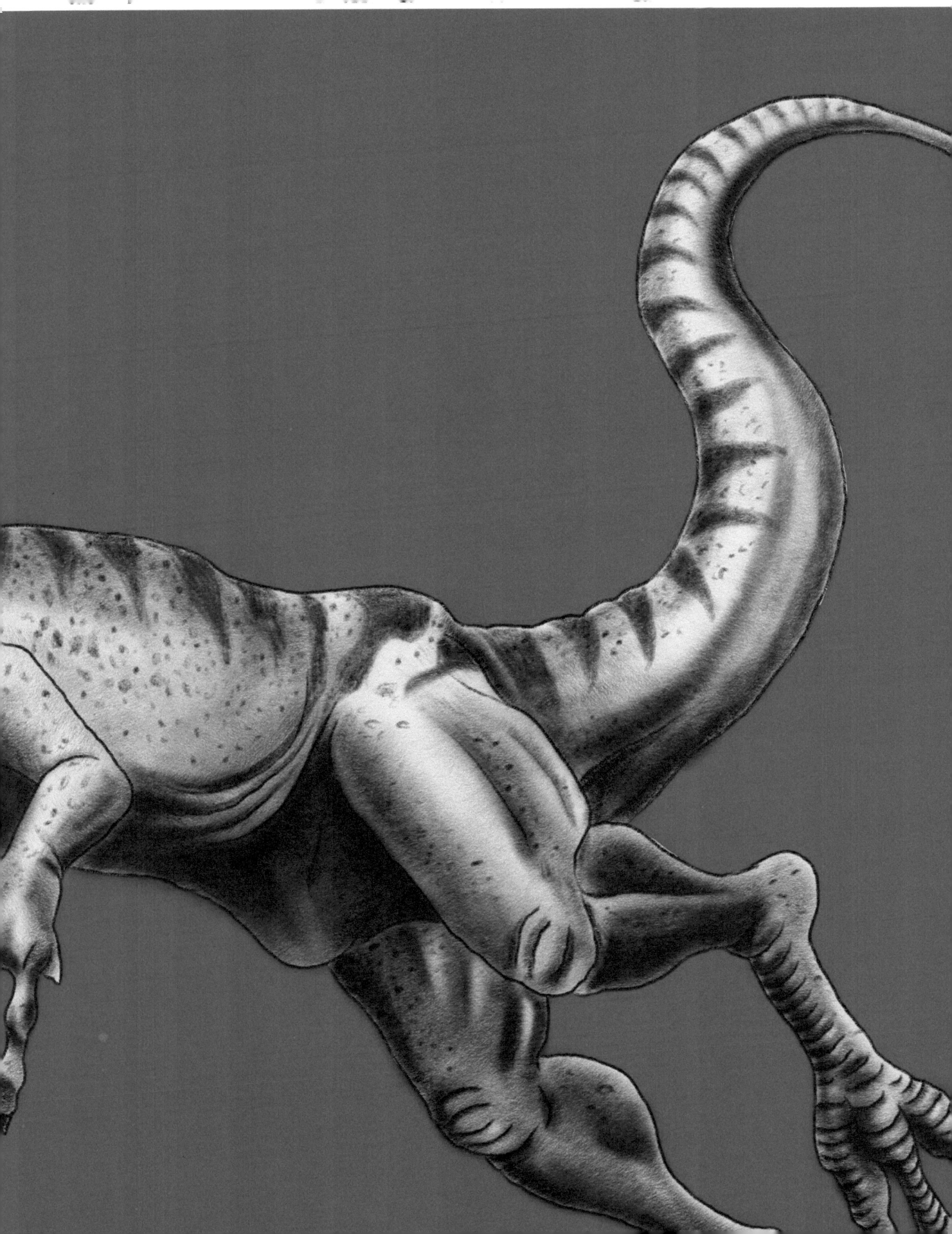

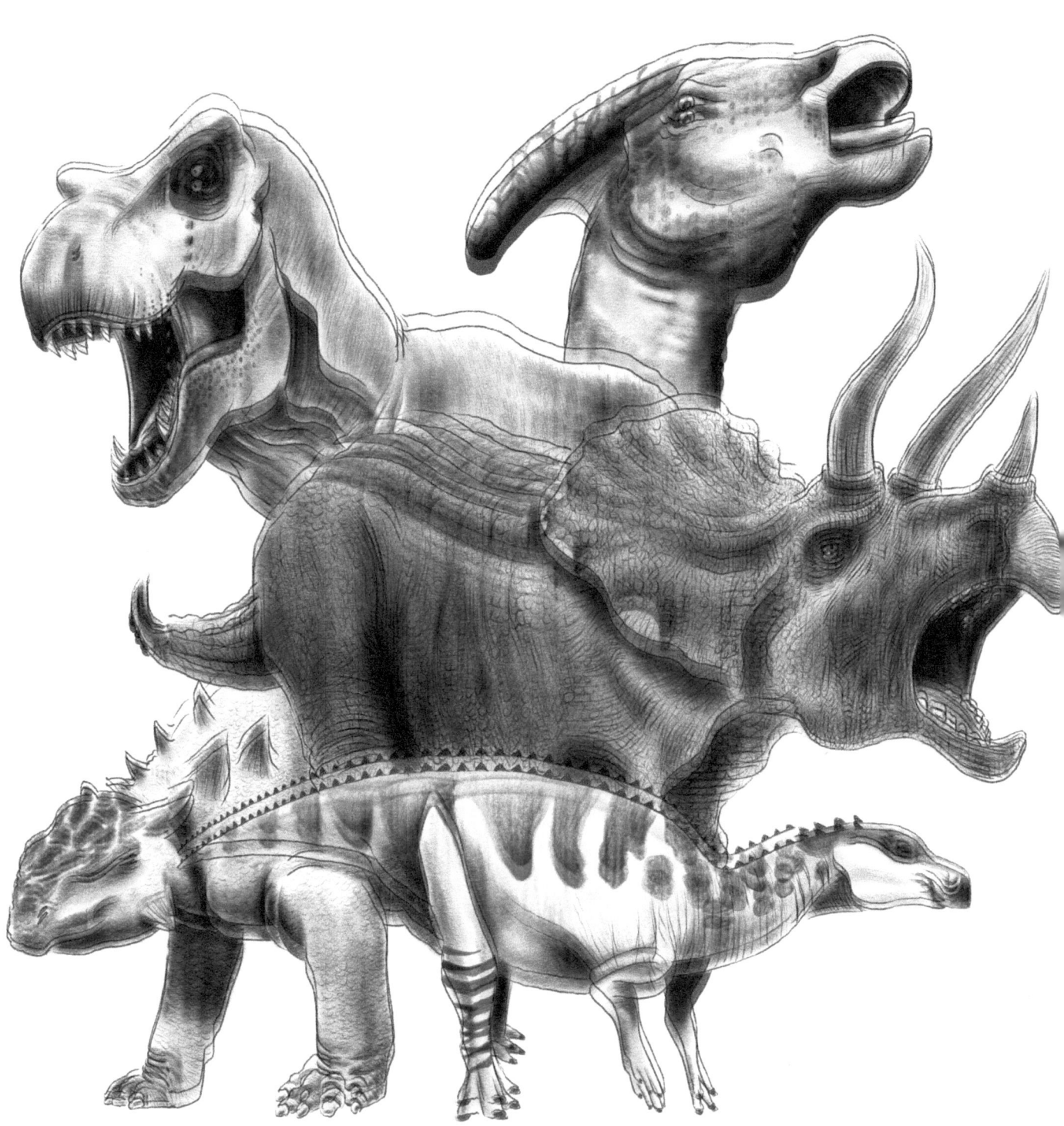

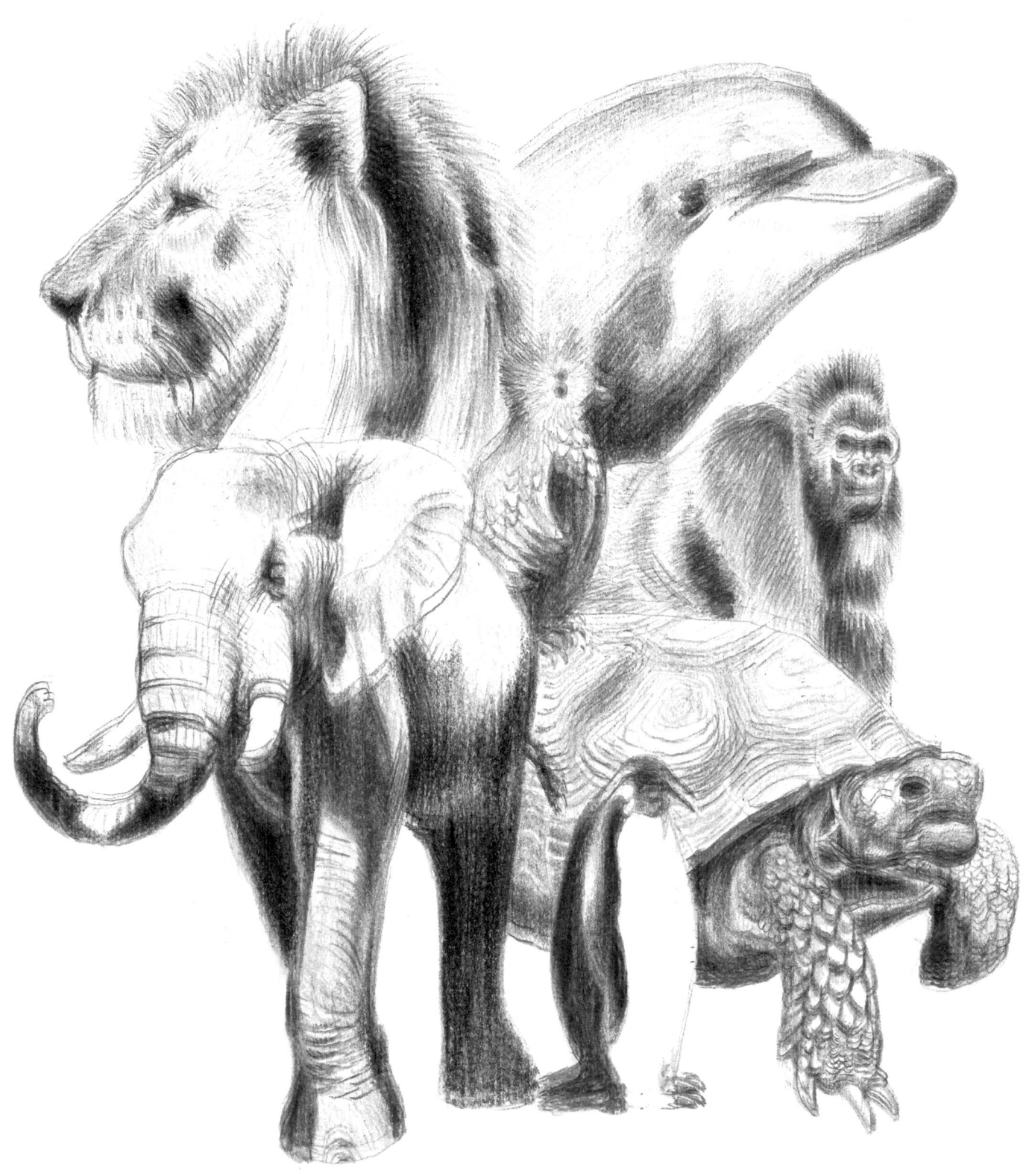

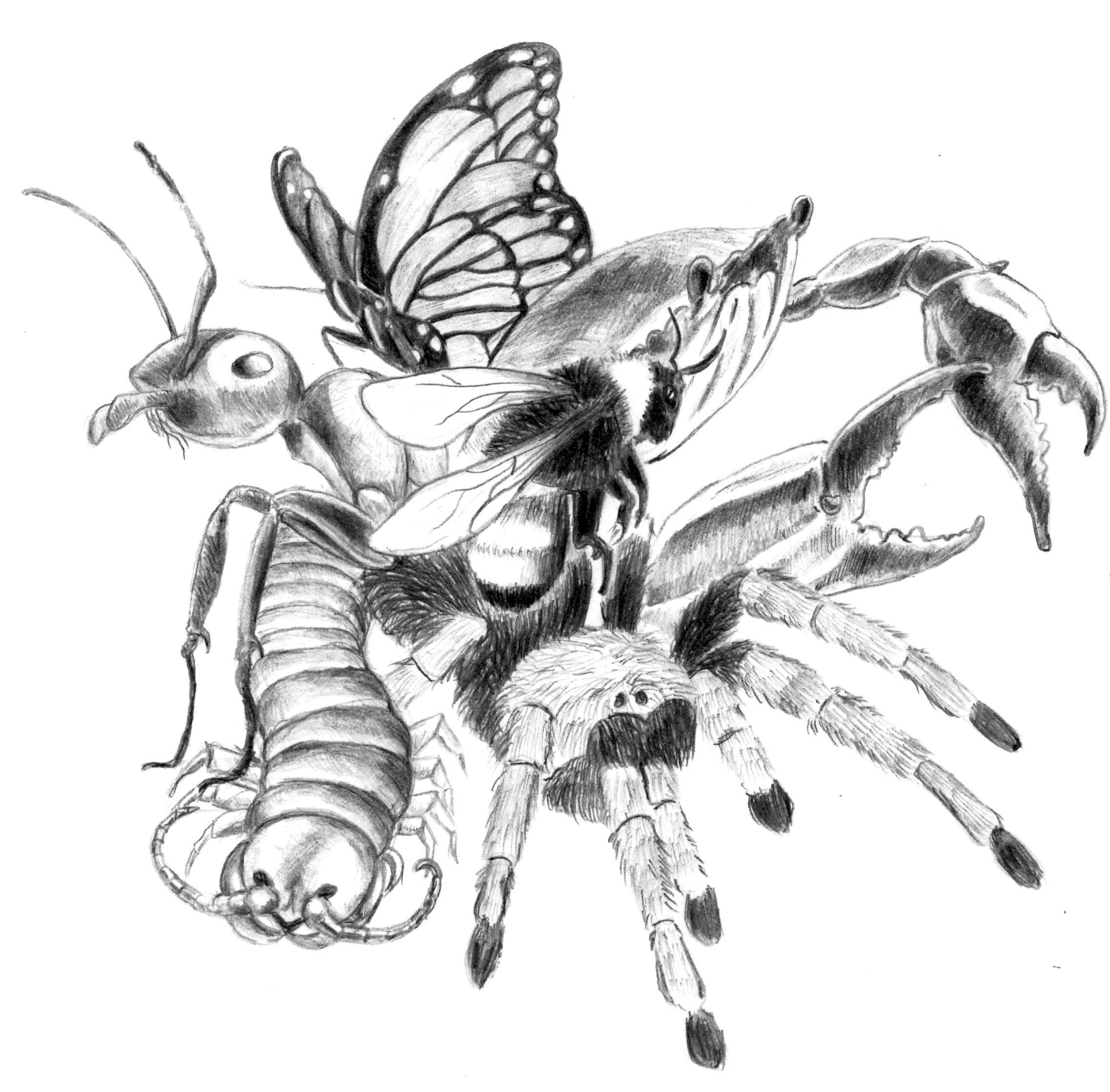

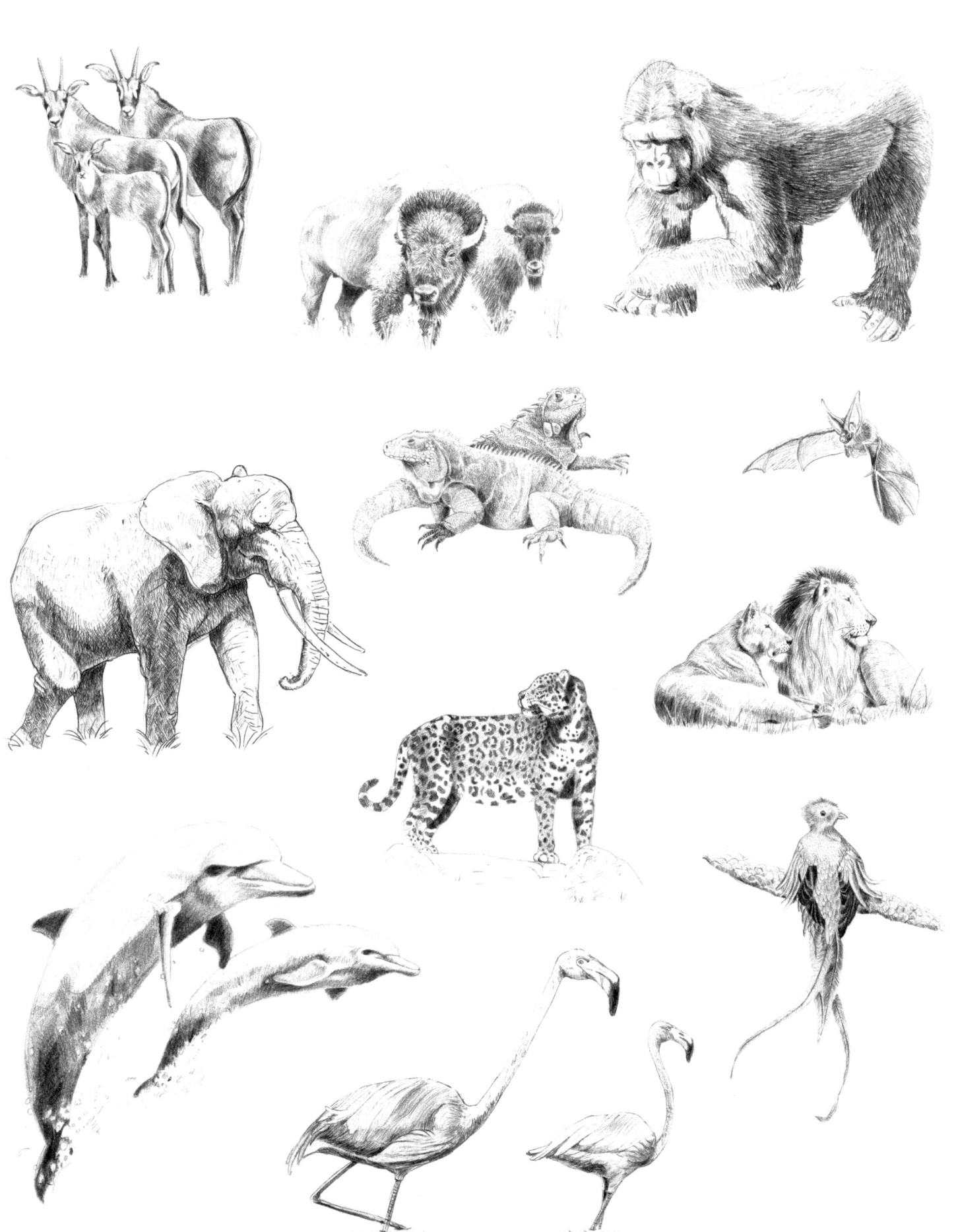

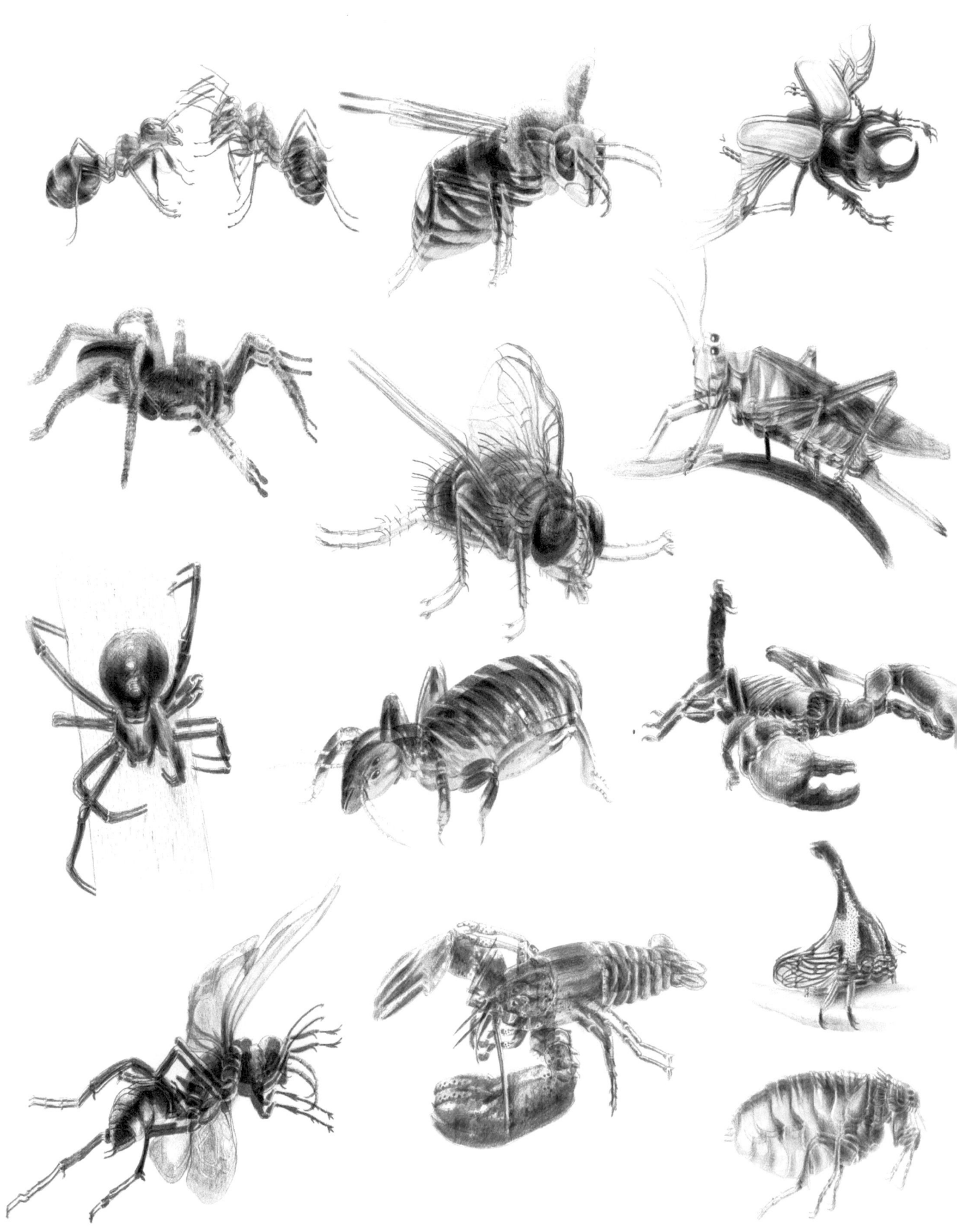

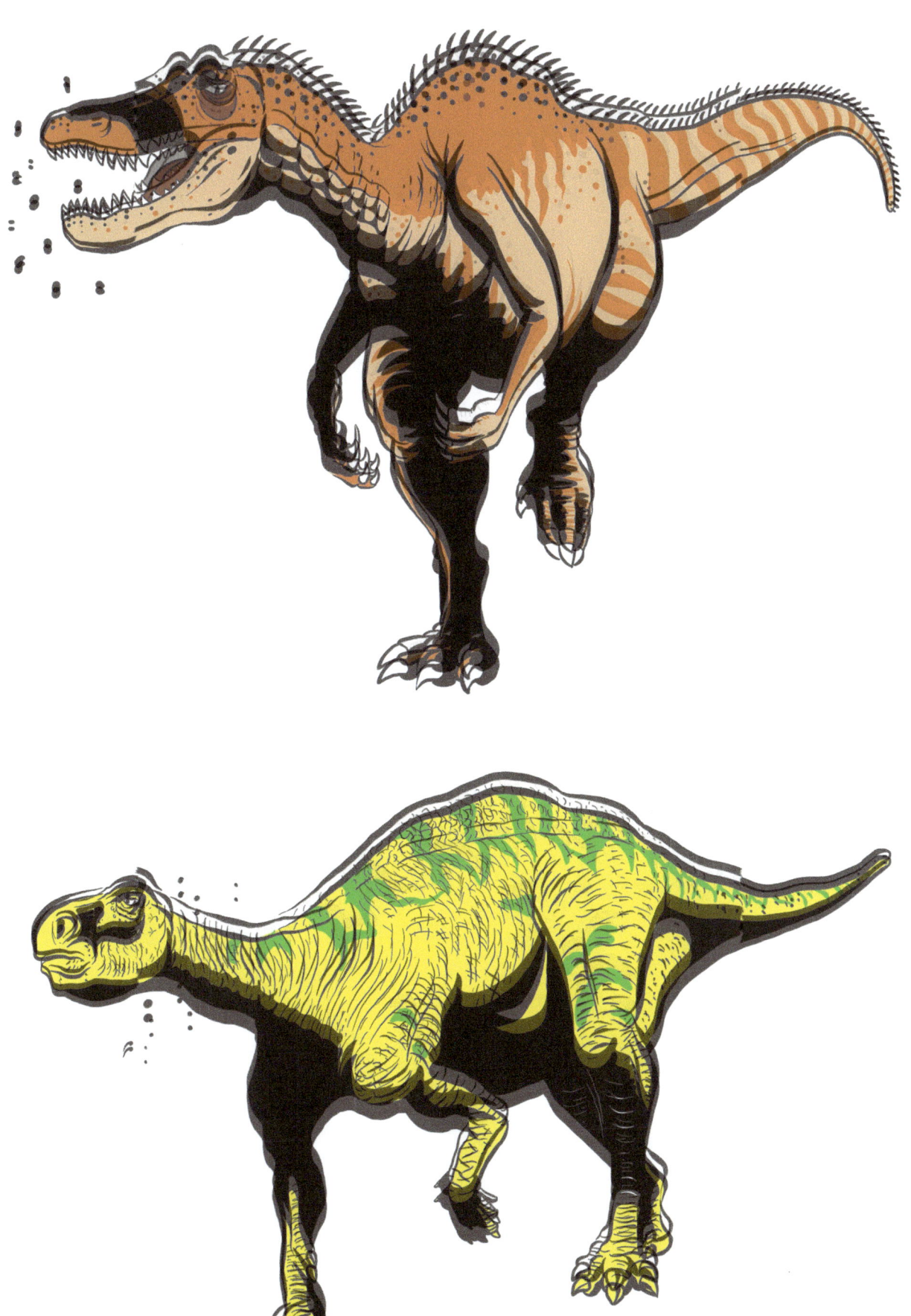

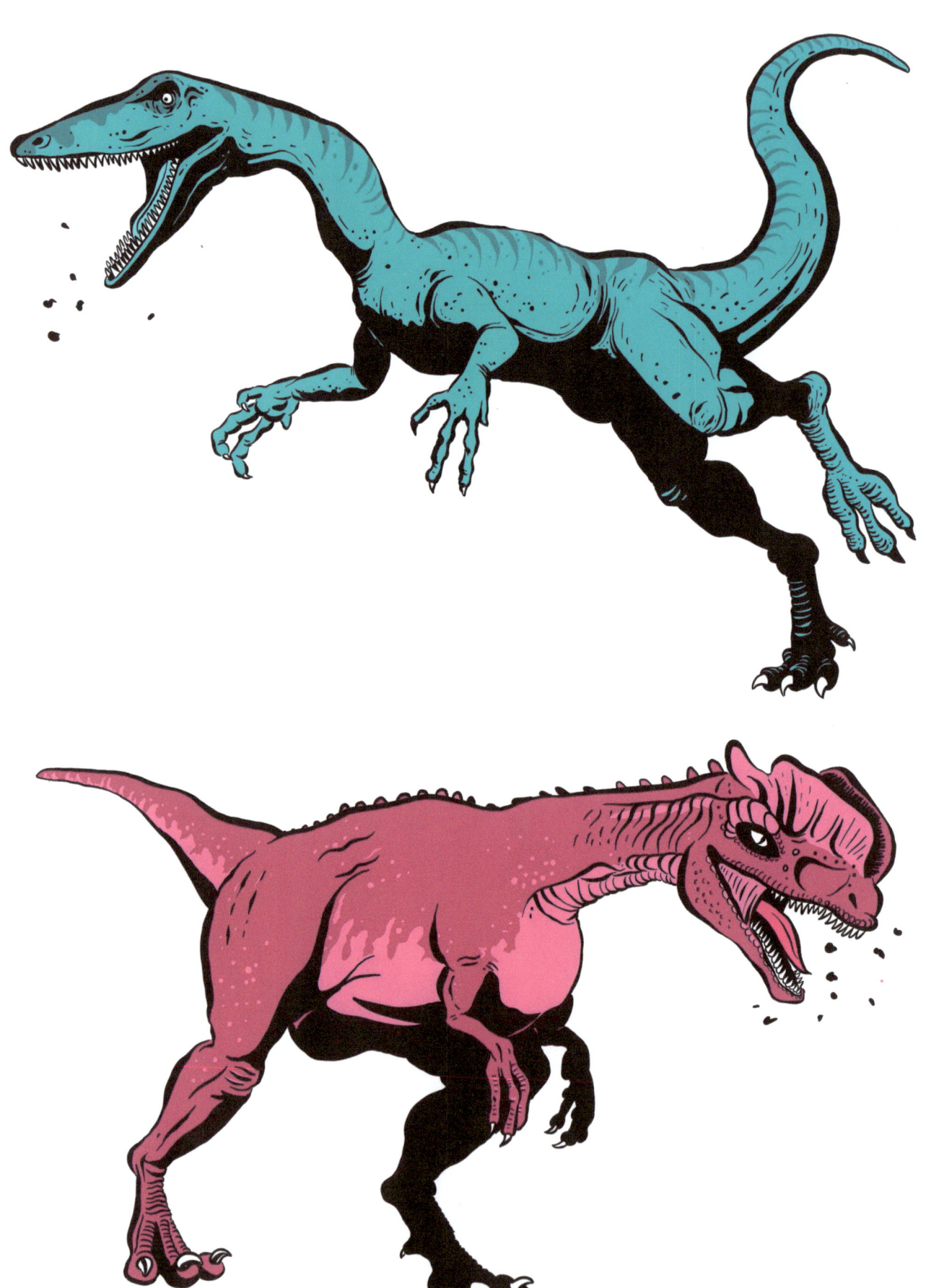

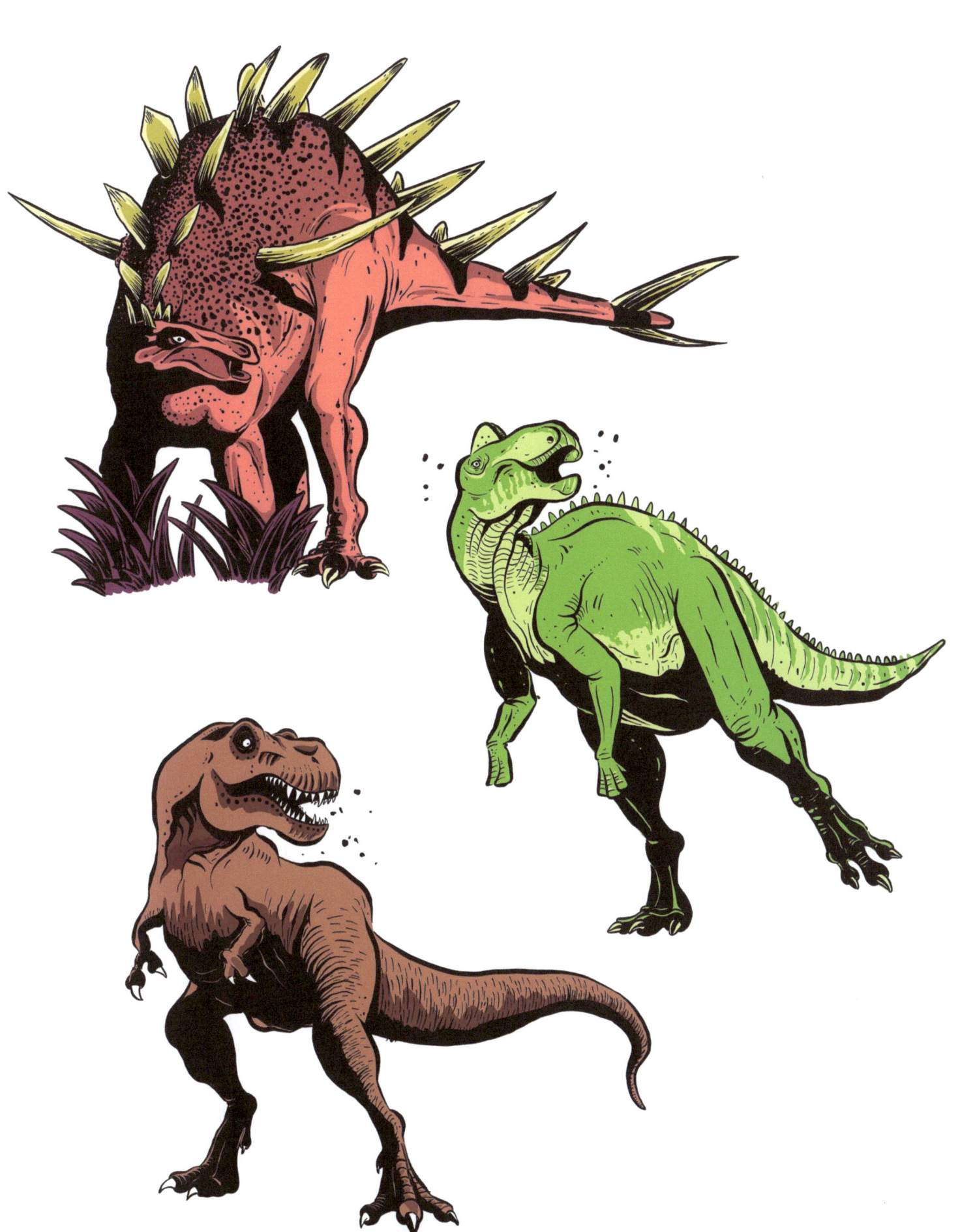

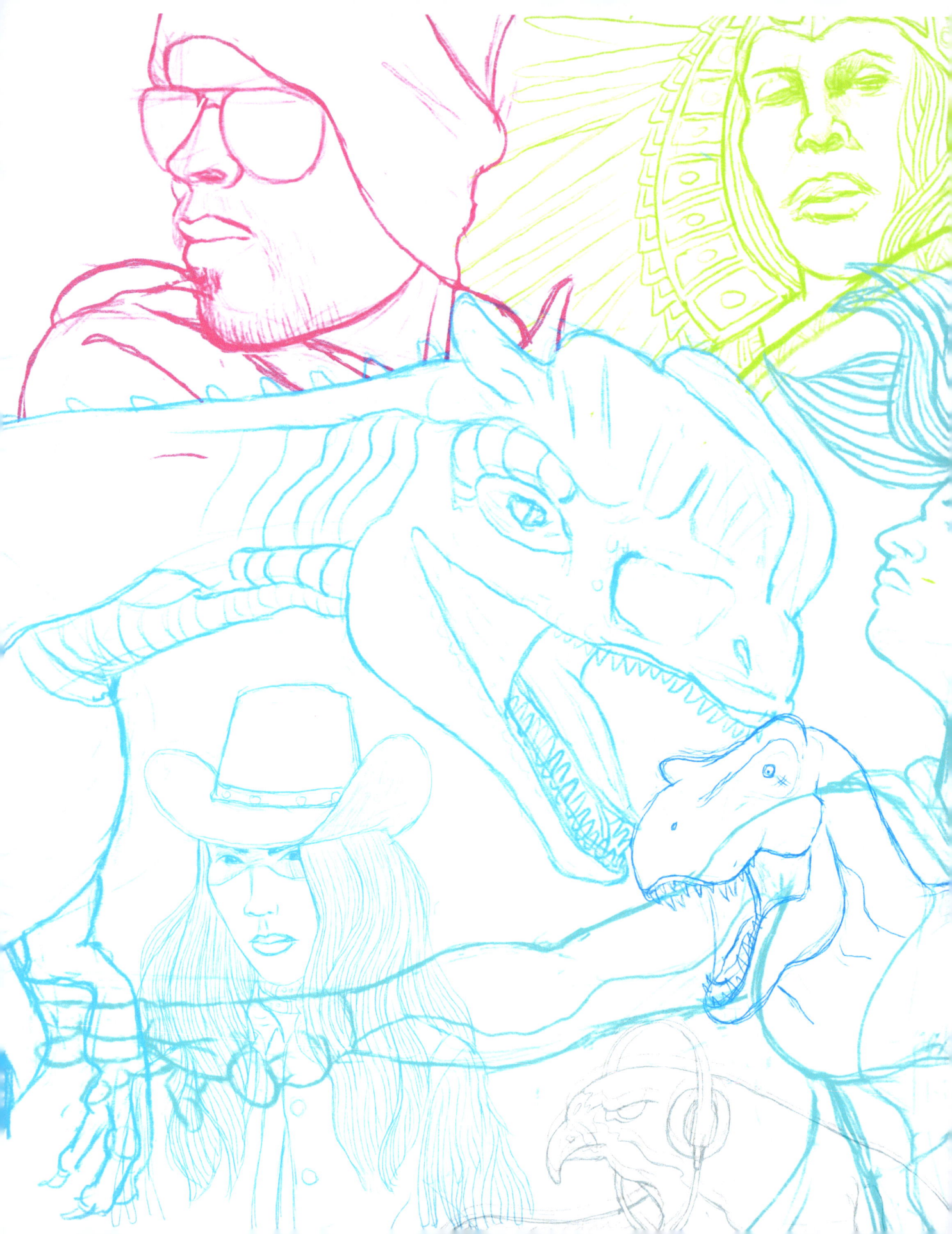

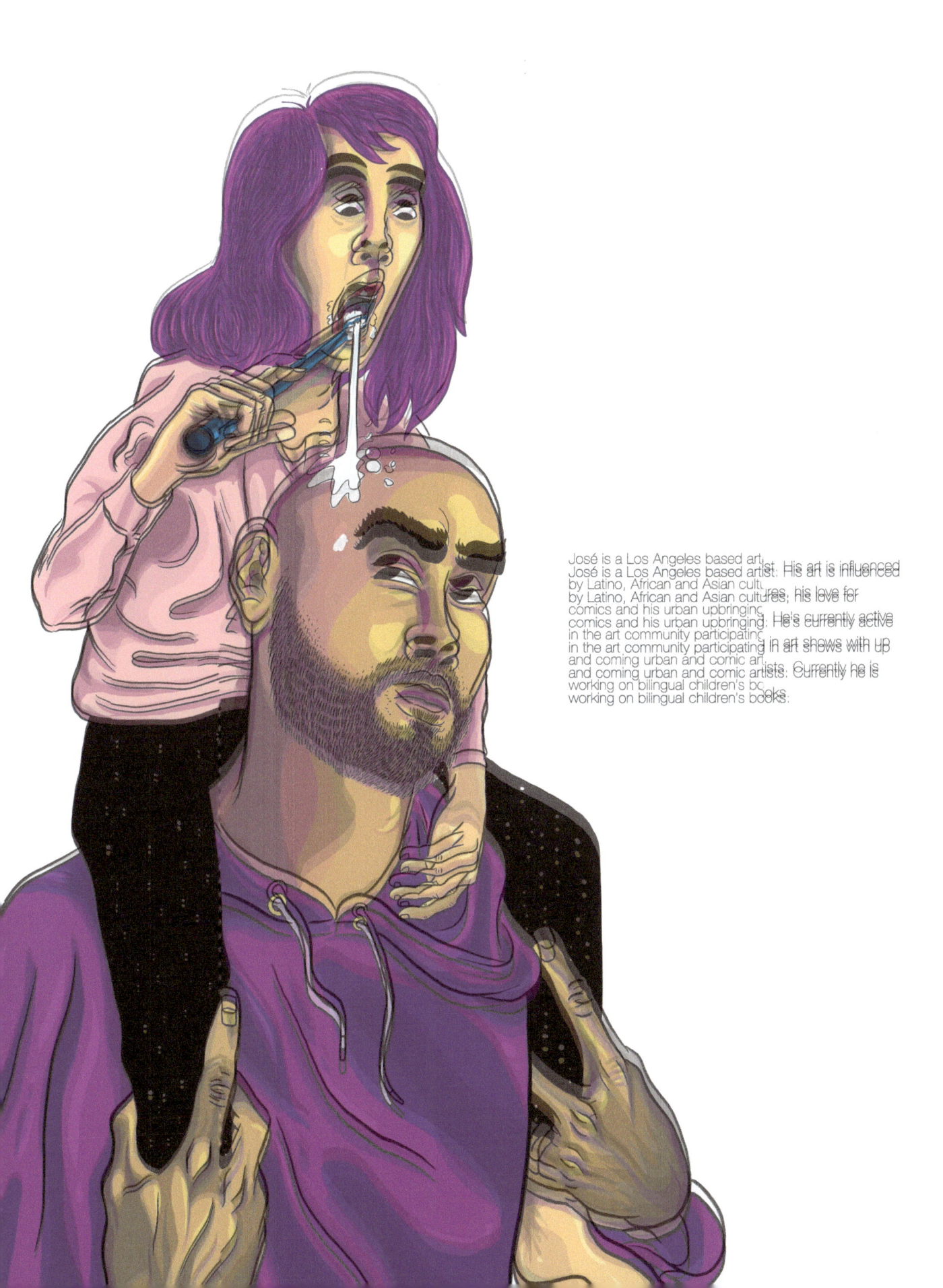

José is a Los Angeles based artist. His art is influenced by Latino, African and Asian cultures; his love for comics and his urban upbringing. He's currently active in the art community participating in art shows with up and coming urban and comic artists. Currently he is working on bilingual children's books.

www.ingramcontent.com/pod-product-compliance
Lightning Source LLC
Chambersburg PA
CBHW051921210526
45473CB00006B/2095